LEGENDS
AND
TALES

LEGENDS
AND
TALES

ANECDOTAL HISTORIES
OF ST. AUGUSTINE, FLORIDA

KAREN HARVEY

the
History
CHARLESTON PRESS LONDON

Published by The History Press
18 Percy Street
Charleston, SC 29403
866.223.5778
www.historypress.net

Front cover: The St. Augustine Saints, a professional baseball team in St. Augustine in the 1940s. *Courtesy of the St. Augustine Historical Society*

Back cover: Bert Hernandez, fondly known as the "strongest man in town" holds his catch of the day. *Courtesy of Mr. and Mrs. Bert Hernandez Jr.*

First published 2005

Manufactured in the United Kingdom

ISBN 1.59629.060.9

Library of Congress Cataloging-in-Publication Data

Harvey, Karen G., 1944-
  Legends and tales : anecdotal histories of St. Augustine, Florida / Karen
Harvey.
     p. cm.
  ISBN 1-59629-060-9 (alk. paper)
1. Saint Augustine (Fla.)--History--Anecdotes. 2. Saint Augustine
(Fla.)--Biography--Anecdotes. I. Title.
  F319.S2H38 2005
  975.9'18--dc22
                          2005011713

Notice: The information in this book is true and complete to the best of our knowledge. It is offered without guarantee on the part of the author or The History Press. The author and The History Press disclaim all liability in connection with the use of this book.

CONTENTS

ACKNOWLEDGEMENTS

The *St. Augustine Record* deserves thanks for being the first publication to bring these stories to the public.

I also thank Charles Tingley and the staff at the St. Augustine Historical Society research library for their significant help locating old photographs or supplying substitutes for those lost over time. And thanks to Sandy Stratton, an adopted Minorcan who loves St. Augustine's history, for all the scrambling she did in retracing my tracks looking for photos—and for her computer mastery in scanning images to printable form.

INTRODUCTION

St. Augustine, Florida, is a city steeped in history and blessed with storytellers. I met many of the fine folks who participated in the "Legends and Tales" series when I embarked on my first publication about my adopted town, *St. Augustine and St. Johns County: A Pictorial History*. I carried their stories with me like a cozy shawl around my shoulders, wanting to share that warmth by passing along the stories through the printed word. When I approached the local newspaper, the *St. Augustine Record*, they welcomed the idea and I began a series that ran periodically from 1988 to 1992. I did not use the traditional oral history paradigm of asking a series of pre-selected questions. Instead I simply let the interviewee reminisce with minimal guidance, hoping to capture the voice of the speaker. The results were often surprising. In order to enrich the stories I prefaced each with an introduction to the individual and added an epilogue, gently smoothing any technical bumps by providing additional information and dates. In this book, the original date of the interview is given, along with current information about the people and places described.

As can be expected, most of the taletellers are no longer with us. One is, however. Elliott Maguire agreed to meet with me again and gave me an update on the turpentine industry he spoke about so eloquently about fifteen years ago. We drove down county roads where developments now sprout in place of trees. In a gentle and resigned manner he explained that today the land is worth only what developers pay for it. The days of farming, turpentining and wood pulp production are over. The message touched me as we stood on a newly cleared dirt road. Mr. Maguire pointed to the tall, healthy pines on both sides of the road and calmly explained, "These are the trees I planted twenty-five years ago." That cycle of production and replenishment has ended and Mr. Maguire understood that.

These stories are a link to the past. I am extremely pleased The History Press recognized their value and suggested printing them in book form. The newspaper versions I keep in plastic bins are of no use to anyone except me. I feel now that these stories are in book form, our link to the past will be preserved. I hope readers will enjoy these legends and tales told by the people who helped shape this wonderful city and county.

A BRIEF NOTE ON
St. Augustine's history

St. Augustine is the nation's oldest city. Properly said, it is "the oldest permanently established European settlement in the continental United States." It was established in 1565 by Pedro Menendez de Aviles of Spain. With the exception of twenty years of British rule from 1763 to 1784, the Spanish presence dominated.

In order to easily explain the unique history of the area, residents often refer to specific time periods:

First Spanish Period 1565–1763
British Decades 1763–1784
The Second Spanish Regime 1784–1821
Territorial Days and Early Statehood 1821–1888
Golden Era of Henry M. Flagler 1888–1914

St. Augustine's most precious landmark is the Castillo de San Marcos, a national monument since 1924. It was completed in 1695 and stands beside the harbor as the oldest stone fort in the United States. More than three centuries old, it has witnessed numerous changes of flags while playing an important part in United States' history.

The Matanzas River runs between the mainland and Anastasia Island. The river received its name from the massacre in 1565 of the French Huguenots by the Spanish Catholics.

In 1768, during the British Period, a group of Mediterranean travelers arrived in Florida as indentured servants. Brought from the Balearic island of Minorca, as well as Italy, Greece and Corsica, the group dwindled from the approximately fourteen hundred that left Minorca to a few hundred who finally escaped from the horrors of the indigo plantation in New Smyrna. This group of Minorcans stayed in Florida for the return of the Spanish and remained when the Americans arrived in 1821. They form the core group of St. Augustine's ancestral residents.

Courtesy of Peggy Davis Saz

COUNTY SHERIFF
L.O. Davis

L.O. Davis served as county sheriff in St. Augustine for twenty-one years, but his prominence extends beyond that admirable accomplishment. L.O. and his relatives have been involved in politics, business, sports and education in St. Augustine and St. Johns County since L.O.'s father's time. The extended family has resided on the same property in West Augustine since his grandparents moved to Whitney Street in 1896. Best of all, L.O. loves to tell stories—and here are some.

THE DOG WITH A SENSE OF HUMOR

Once I was going out quail hunting with Irvin Drysdale—of the Alligator Farm, you know? He had a five-shot Browning and he said as we were going out, "When the dog points today I want y'all to just leave your guns in the car. I want to show you how to shoot quail. I'll show you how to kill five birds on the rise."

So, when we got out to the countryside, the dog came running around a palmetto patch and was going pretty fast. He didn't smell the birds and he got right in the middle of them before he realized where he was and before he could point. But the problem was he couldn't point standing up because the quail would see him, so he just lay down on his side.

Drys goes up and looks at the dog and says, "L.O., the dog's snake bit or had a stroke."

So I said, "You think so?" and I went up to the dog and reached down to move him and these quail flew up all around me and all around Drys. Of course it frightened him just as it would anyone else. But he emptied the shotgun—shot five times. The dog's standing there looking to see if anything fell. Nothing fell so the dog looks at us and then trots out and picks up a pine burr and brings it back and hands it to Drys.

Drys said, "I'm gonna kill him. I'm gonna kick his head off. He's making fun of me. He can't make fun of me like that."

Yes, sir, that old dog knew what he was doing right along. You can't tell me bird dogs don't have a sense of humor.

The hunter in the story, Mr. W.I. Drysdale, was an owner of the Alligator Farm on Anastasia Island, a business he purchased in 1937 with F. Charles Usina. For many years the prominent resident was president of the St. Augustine Historical Society.

DEPRESSION DAYS

The Depression really wasn't felt so badly here. There was always plenty of mullet fishing. We'd all sit around a fire eating mullet. There definitely was plenty of food. I used to go to Summer Haven and fish from the Matanzas Bridge. At first I went on the mail boat that was run by Captain Joe Sanchez. For a while I kept a sixteen-foot skiff down at Summer Haven and used to go out with Sunny Noel.

Speaking of rowboats, do you know who we called the strongest man in the world? It was Bert Hernandez—one of the greatest Minorcans ever lived. He used to row all the way from the yacht pier to the Matanzas Inlet almost every day. He'd fish by Fort Matanzas or by Devil's Elbow [south of the Crescent Beach Bridge]. He kept a log of his catches and would know exactly where to catch the most fish and which ones he could find. He sold his fish to Salvador's Fish Market and made a lot of money that way.

Anyway, during the Depression we had plenty of fish. And, oh yes, turtle eggs. I used to hitch a ride from the bridge, say ten or ten thirty at night and go about twelve miles to the other side of the hammock and walk back to Summer Haven. I'd get back around five in the morning, sometimes after sunrise. Nighttime is the best time for collecting turtle eggs. I could sell them for ten cents a dozen. By the way, do you know what the biggest threat to turtles was back then? Seagulls. The seagulls would eat the baby turtles

L.O. Davis contemplates a hunting or fishing tale. *Courtesy of Peggy Davis Saz*

before they could get to the ocean. We could eat all the turtle eggs we wanted and not endanger the turtles.

The other thing I loved to catch was stone crabs. I could get as high as six dozen stone crabs in one evening and sell those for $2.06 a dozen. We would have to dive for them. You know, a stone crab a lot of times will live around pilings. Mostly, though, they live in shell banks and at low tide the holes are only three or four feet underwater. On the inland waterway there was a good place where there is a sharp step off and as you came along the bank you could feel the holes with your hands. You could dive down and take your hand and slide it right over his back. Then you turn him sideways and pull him out, because if you don't turn him he'll dig his claws in the side of the bank and you can't budge him. Don't put your thumb down. Just slide your hand over. I never was bitten, but if you do get bitten what you do is relax the minute he bites you and he'll turn you lose. It's very hard to keep from jerking, but if you jerk, well, then he hangs on. I've never seen it but they say that turtles can stick their head in there and catch that stone crab and eat him.

Then, you know, we always had the farmers out in the county. They'd come in from Mill Creek and trade for the fish. We didn't always need money to keep from being hungry. We'd trade fish for potatoes or vegetables and everyone could eat.

My father always gave one cupful of wheat, grits or rice to the poorer people that came into his grocery store. We took care of each other. There was a Jewish merchant, Mr. Snyder, who was very generous to people in need. I remember that once he gave groceries to people who were sheltered in the armory during a storm. And, you know what else he did? He gave meat to St. Joseph's Academy all during the Depression and never charged them a dime.

My mother, too, did what she could. She kept a pot of soup on the stove for hobos that would come by. She was always ready to feed a hungry mouth. Yes, life during the Depression wasn't so bad here in St. Johns County.

According to journalist and historian Robert Dow's assessment of Depression days in St. Augustine ("Yesterday and the Day Before" in *The Oldest City: St. Augustine Saga Of Survival*, published by the St. Augustine Historical Society in 1983), L.O. Davis's memories are right on target. Although some small businesses and farmers were hurt by the Depression, the majority of the residents fared well. There were no soup kitchens or bread lines here. St. Augustinians preferred to take care of their own and did exactly that by sharing what they could. The fishing industry did indeed stay strong and tourism during the summer months actually increased.

West Augustine school

This building here on Madison Street is where I went to school until I was nine or ten years old. Let me tell you about this one boy who the police had to drag to school every day. This boy was only in third grade but he was about thirteen or fourteen years old. He hated school and his parents had to call the police to make him go there. One day the police brought him in to the school in handcuffs and cuffed him to the desk. But the boy carried the desk outside and smashed it to pieces and ran away again.

Another day the boy was in the classroom and wanted to go to the bathroom. The teacher wouldn't let him go so he walked over to the corner of the room and p——— right there. That boy was so mean he hit me once and broke my arm. It was about then my folks decided to send me over to Orange Street School where I went until I finished grade school.

And we think our educational problems are new! The building that prompted Mr. Davis's recollection of his school days is located at 8–10 Madison Street, formerly School Street. It was built between 1905 and 1910 and housed the New Augustine School until the 1920s, when Evelyn Hamblen was constructed and referred to as the West Augustine Grammar School.

January 14, 1988

In 2005, the old school still stands. Abandoned and deteriorating, it remains a link to the past that L.O. remembered in 1988.

Courtesy of the St. Augustine Historical Society

THE EARLY DAYS OF BASEBALL
Charles Colee

C harles Colee is a native of St. Augustine with roots extending to the Minorcan and Spanish settlers. For years he organized the Royal Family pageants and activities and was an advocate of preserving St. Augustine's heritage. Colee fondly remembers the St. Augustine Saints, seen above.

St. Augustine in the 1920s and 1930s was quite a baseball town. At that time St. Augustine headed the Florida State League, which was amateur at first and later went into semi-pro playing and, as I say, the entire city was very enthusiastic. In fact, on Wednesdays the stores used to close. I remember that every Wednesday during the summer businesses closed so the players could compete and spectators could go watch. And everyone did go watch—the stadium was always packed.

The teams played in Lewis Park. Now, Lewis Park was located just south of Flagler Hospital and was named after someone related to the Flagler family. That was when we had the trolley service that ran down Central Avenue [now Martin Luther King Street]. It started at the water works, which is now the Women's Club [today The Garden Center], went down San Marco up to King Street and down Central Avenue. One destination was Lewis Field and it was something to see those cars just loaded with baseball people hanging out the back.

The whole thing started with people in the community playing against each other—always on Wednesday afternoons. Later we played teams from Palatka, Sanford, Fernandina and other cities around here. You know what the Sanford team was called? The "Celery-Feds" because that was where all the celery was grown. We were called the St. Augustine Saints. The Palatka Pals were our biggest rivals and fights would break out when we played each other. We won most of the time, though. There was also a time when we played the big leagues in exhibition games. The picture I have was taken in 1923 when the Saints played the Washington Senators. They tell me some big league teams trained in St. Augustine, but I don't remember any.

I remember once when the stadium burned. The Saints had a game the next day or shortly thereafter. Like I say, civic pride was so great the team had to do something, so they borrowed convict uniforms—yes, convict uniforms from the county jail. They played in black-and-white striped uniforms with the little caps on their heads. It didn't bother them any—St. Augustine has always thrived on gimmicks and promotions.

Another time I remember the stadium lights failed. We were near the end of the game and something had to be done. There were maybe twenty-five or thirty cars parked around the field, so the drivers formed them in a circle around the stadium and turned on the headlights and we finished the game that way.

For a while during the war years we didn't play much baseball here. Then, after about 1945 interest picked up again and teams were formed on a semi-pro or professional basis. Yes, baseball has always been important to St. Augustine. After a while Fred Francis Field was built and teams are still playing there and on Joe James Field and drawing lots of fans. Baseball is St. Augustine's game.

Baseball was indeed an important game to this already sport-loving city. Throughout the summers the Saints kept ball fans excited with their games against neighboring teams. They vied with the Florida East Coast Clerks for the city championship title and challenged teams from as far away as Waycross and Brunswick, Georgia. The Saints played the semi-professional teams from Lake City and Titusville, maintaining an exceptionally good record against all opposition. It appears, however, from an analysis of the *St. Augustine Record*'s sports pages in the mid-1920s that playing the Palatka Pals was the most exciting challenge. One headline exclaims that the Saints will play their "Ancient Foes." Another boldly boasts: "Saints Smother Pals."

Baseball was played on Lewis Field at the south end of Marine Street. Flagler Hospital can be seen in the background. *Courtesy of the St. Augustine Historical Society*

In 1923 and 1924 the *St. Augustine Record* proudly announced exhibition games against the Cincinnati Reds, who apparently were here for spring training. In 1923 the line-up for one game was as follows: Matzet, catcher; Stanley Colee, first base; "Boots" Wolfe, second base; Freddie Francis, short stop; Fred Oldfather, third base; and Cliff Colee, Sam McDaniels and Bobbie Small at outfield. The headlines for this Saturday game ran: "SAINTS HOLD REDS TO LOW SCORE TIE." The teams tied at 2 and Cliff Colee was complimented on his pitching (even though he was listed as an outfielder). The next year the Reds trounced the Saints 5 to 1. The *Cincinnati Enquirer* had nice things to say about the team, however, in the following commentary: "The Reds closed their long campaign in the play-ground state by trimming the strong semi-pro club known as the Saints in a fast contest this afternoon by the score of 5 to 1. The local team is a powerful organization in which the citizens of the Oldest City take laudable pride, considering it is stronger than the teams in the Florida State League."

Lewis Field, with its ample grandstand and convenient clubhouse, apparently was attractive to other major league teams for spring training as well. In addition to the Reds, the Newark Bears used the facilities for pre-season play. *Record* articles in 1930 mention the Bears as spring residents with one article describing a game between the Bears and another major league team, the Buffalo Bisons. The Bisons won 5 to 3.

I am sure everyone in the city was proud of the performances of Mr. Charles Colee's relatives in those early days of baseball and we can all delight in the memories of those sun-filled, fun-filled summers around the baseball diamond.

January 21, 1988

In 1990, Flagler Hospital facilities were moved to a new, large health complex off Route 1 South and State Road 312. In later years the building was razed to make way for condominiums.

Courtesy of the St. Augustine Historical Society

BASEBALL IN THE '40S

Red Cox and Larry Hartley

J. Edward "Red" Cox came to St. Augustine in 1946 to play baseball for the Saints, seen above. After one year, however, Red was launched into a forty-one-year career of service to the county with thirty-eight of those years spent as recreation department superintendent.

Larry Hartley is a St. Augustine native with deep roots and lots of kin, many of whom have held prestigious positions in the community throughout the years. Mr. Hartley played baseball for the Saints right out of high school.

RED COX

I came down here after World War II. It was in February—about the fifteenth or sixteenth. I had to try out with Bill Steinecke who was manager at that time. Hiram Favor, who was county clerk for many, many years, was in the service with me and he mentioned my name to Tony Meitin, who was on the board of directors of the Saints. We used the old practice field. Before World War II, baseball was played down at Lewis Field—on Marine Street near Flagler Hospital. We played many, many years down there. But because of the activities, particularly going to night ball, they had to move from the hospital because of the lights. So Mr. Francis built Francis Field out there at the old recreation field on Castillo Drive. They probably kept on playing on Lewis Field during the daytime. I've talked to some old-timers and they said you couldn't believe the attendance in those years before the war. The people would go down on Wednesday afternoon. They told me they closed all the stores a half a day to go down there and play. One of the biggest rivals was Palatka, they say. In 1946, the year I played, the team drew over seventy-two thousand people.

LARRY HARTLEY

I started playing right after high school. I played for Bill Steinecke. I only played here one year and then went to Korea during the war. Then when I came out of the army I played on several AAA teams. That's the league just under the majors. I played for Denver, North Carolina, Hartford, Connecticut, and Atlanta. Finally I signed with the Milwaukee Braves.

I want to go back to one thing. Red was talking about the ball field down at Flagler Hospital. When I was a little teeny kid my dad used to love to go there. Down there they didn't have any fences, just cedar trees. They had one guy by the name of Tom Mash—he was a left-handed hitter, and I mean when he'd come up they'd expect him to hit home runs every time. And when he'd get one and it would go over those trees it would look like it was going twenty miles out. People used to laugh, you know. A home run wasn't over the fence. It was over the cedar trees.

Back then the Florida State League was a class D league. In those days they had D, C, B, AA and AAA. This was professional baseball, but minor league. See, nowadays they don't have D, C and B; professional baseball starts at A. They have a rookie league, they call it. Back in those days in most of the states around here there were numerous teams from D on up. And in those days when you got to AA or higher you were considered an outstanding ball player. And that's the reason I say today they've gone from the power hitters, and good all around ball players, strictly to speed. In those days there was nobody in the major leagues [that couldn't hit]. The greatest fielders in the world could hit .280 and above. Now you see a lot of .200 hitters in the major leagues. That's disgraceful. Back then you had to work your way up. You know what I mean? You didn't just step into the big leagues. You had to pull yourself up and you got better as you went. You earned your way up through the leagues. You had more of them so you could learn as you went up.

RED COX

You know, when you had D ballplayers when Larry and I was playing, there were many of them that would be big league players today.

LARRY HARTLEY

I go up and watch AA in [name deleted] and I'm embarrassed. I sit there and think when I tell people, "Well, I played AA ball." And people will say, "That's not too high."

Francis Field, shown in this aerial photo, is nestled between Orange Street and West Castillo Drive. It was named for sportsman Freddy Francis. *Courtesy of the St. Augustine Historical Society*

But I guarantee you our class D ball club—right here—could have given anything I've seen in [name deleted] *a fit. I mean—I'm not bragging or anything—but it was a whole different brand of baseball.*

Bill Steinecke came down here to manage the team and he went all over to get players. He'd sign up these players for the Saints. He really knew his ball players. So he just went out to find what he wanted. He had one from Puerto Rico or someplace. I don't know where he found that one. He'd get them from anywhere—shipyards, anywhere. But, anyway, lots of them were real good and worked their way up from here. We had numerous ball players that could have made it to the majors. Lyle Judy was good but he got messed up in a car accident. We had another guy, James Smith, who was an outstanding pitcher. He should have gone to the majors but, like I say, there were so many outstanding ball players you just had to sit and wait your turn. Stan Corpinsky—he pitched later in the major leagues.

RED COX

One of the funniest things I remember was one of our bus trips. We were coming back from Deland or Sanford and Jack Wilks, our third baseman, was driving the bus. And there he is driving along and suddenly he puts the breaks on and there was all this cattle in the road. They had open fence laws back then and here we were about eleven in the morning trying to chase the cattle off the highway. We traveled a lot. The league included St. Augustine, Deland, Sanford, Daytona Beach, Leesburg and Orlando, so we had a lot of driving to do.

LARRY HARTLEY

I remember Orlando and Leesburg were our worst trips. Nowadays you don't even think about it because we have all these fancy highways. But then you had to go on all those little back roads. What it was, he [Jack Wilks] made a few extra bucks driving that bus. He played third base and he played everything with his body. He was about as big around as he was tall and he'd hold his glove off to one side and he'd let the ball hit him and it would bounce off him. He'd catch it and throw them out. He was a great third baseman.

But the only thing I can say, on our Saints ball club—Red would remember—we had Indians. We had two Indians. We had a Puerto Rican. Then we had Sili Yoker that year. They'd always pull us up. You never knew when you went to the locker room, or when you were sitting on the bench, somebody—everybody chewed tobacco—and you'd be sitting there and if you weren't careful pretty soon there'd be a great big wad of chewing tobacco on your shoes—all over. And they'd hide your glove. We had a great bunch. They came from all over. I tell you I don't know where Bill Steinecke found them all. What a mixture!

RED COX

The team finally disbanded in the 1950s. I think it was because of television. Everybody stayed home and watched television.

LARRY HARTLEY

Yes, that's a good point. Baseball was a big thing back then—before TV. Everyone in town talked about it. You didn't have all these outside activities and stuff going on. Why, you could barely find a place to park when you went to the games.

RED COX

If you didn't go to the ball park as soon as you got off work or at least by six o'clock—the games started at seven o'clock—you'd have to park your car down past where the old city building was. People were standing in line. It sure isn't like that any more.

During the war years of the 1940s the popular St. Augustine Saints semi-professional baseball team was disbanded and the sports pages of the *Record* no longer touted the team's victories nor lamented its losses. In 1946, however, William (Bill) Steinecke was enticed to move to St. Augustine to manage a newly forming professional Saints team. Bill Steinecke's baseball career began in Lawrence, Massachusetts, in 1926. The catcher played in leagues from Seattle to Texas to Pittsburgh and more. Steinecke had been with the New York Yankees before coming to St. Augustine. This talented and innovative manager pulled together a team of about forty players, netting any and every skilled sportsman he encountered.

Banner headlines on the sports page of the February 8, 1946 *Record* stated: "Bill Steinecke will manage Saints," and proceeded with accolades: "One of the most colorful figures in minor league baseball will manage the Saints in the Florida State League during the 1946 season. A Saint's uniform won't be new for the hard-slugging catcher, for in 1935 he performed behind the plate for Fred Francis's Saints during the 'gold-plated' days of the fast semi-pro league of that era."

It was March 17, 1946, when the paper notified the public of the pending arrival of Red Cox. "Eddie Cox is major league material. He comes to the Saints with one of the greatest reputations of any service team player in the county. While with the Chatham Field [Georgia] team Cox impressed major and minor league scouts alike with his .330 batting average and his great arm."

Another article dated April 2, 1947, states, "Red Cox continued to show up well behind the plate and sparked his team's offensive with a long home run into deep centerfield in the second inning."

Unfortunately the Saints folded in 1951. Not one player was invited to participate in the 1950 All Star Game and, for whatever reason, that apparently marked the end of professional baseball in St. Augustine.

January 28, 1988

Although Flagler Hospital and Lewis Field no longer exist at the end of Marine Street, the baseball field named for Freddie Francis is still used for sporting events.

Courtesy of Mr. and Mrs. Bert Hernandez Jr.

STRONGEST MAN IN TOWN
Bert Hernandez

STORY TOLD BY SLADE PINKHAM

Slade Pinkham comes from a distinguished St. Augustine family. His father, W.S.M. Pinkham, was a city council member and mayor in 1889. W.S.M. Pinkham Jr. (Slade), also a city council member, was a member of the board of health and the board of public instruction and served as municipal judge. Slade Pinkham worked in the accounting department of the Florida East Coast Railroad for fifty years. Over the years he has touched the lives of city residents as the athletic director of the Osceola Canoe Club, the coach of St. Joseph's girls' basketball team and as a leader in the Catholic church, Catholic parish schools and Knights of Columbus.

He was a boyhood friend of Bert Hernandez who, two years his senior, was Pinkham's idol. This is Slade Pinkham's tribute to his friend Bert Hernandez (seen in the photo above rowing down the Matanzas River).

In the passing of Bert I lost one of my oldest and best friends. Seventy-five years ago Bert lived in the Ocean View Hotel and I lived on Pinkham's dock in front of the Ocean View, where now the Santa Marie restaurant stands. We used to hunt marsh hens in the marsh right across the bay from the Ocean View in what is now Davis Shores.

My father built the Ocean View and the dock in 1884. I was born in the Ocean View in 1901. My mother died in the Ocean View in 1905 and my father sold the hotel to Mr. Henry E. Hernandez, Bert's father, in 1909. The Hernandez family, Mr. and Mrs. Henry Hernandez, Harry, Virgie, Bert, Ruth and Alice then moved into the Ocean View and my father opened a fish market and oyster parlor on the dock.

Bert was one of the best specimens of physical development I have ever known (amateur, I mean). He became interested in bodybuilding at an early age and started using bar bells and other methods of physical development, which he continued throughout most of his life.

He was two years older than me and he always seemed like a big brother. Bert always looked out for me.

I well remember when the water sports were in full swing in the Alcazar pool. All the boys in town that could swim (and about all of them could swim) could join the water sports and take part in the programs on Saturday night. Their reward was that they could use the pool during the week for free.

During the water sports program they had swimming races, high diving, fancy diving and other aquatic events. On one side of the pool there were five or six ropes extending from the rafters with a ring tied to the rope. The ropes were equidistant from each other and the rings were large enough for you to get a handhold. On the other side of the pool at the deep end there was a trapeze extending from the rafters and at the shallow. The idea was to start from the platform at the deep end and swing out on the trapeze, sail through the air feet first and snag the rope and sit on the knot and land on the platform in the shallow end. That was called "swagging." Using the rings was called "going the rings." Bert would not only "go the rings" but he would "roll the rings," somersaulting his body as he swung from rope to rope.

Fishing was Bert's first love. He knew where the fish were, when they would bite and how to catch them. He caught hundreds of pounds, which he ate, gave away or sold to the fish markets. He would not catch fish too small to eat. He would throw them back and let them grow up.

Bert pitched for the Fred Francis Saints baseball team. One day he took Fred fishing in the inlet. This is the story Fred told me about that day. You can believe what you want. They met at the foot of Pinkham's dock where Bert kept his boat.

Fred: "Do you want me to row?"
Bert: "No, you sit down there in the stern. I'll row."
I sat down in the stern and Bert started to row and pretty soon the water started boiling up behind the stern of the boat. We passed two or three motorboats and finally he stopped rowing and threw out the anchor. He looked around and sat down making no effort to fish.

Bert Hernandez holds his catch of the day. *Courtesy of Mr. and Mrs. Bert Hernandez Jr.*

Fred: "Aren't you going to fish?"

Bert: "There's nothing biting now."

Fred: "Well, I'm going to fish."

So I threw out my line and nothing happened. After awhile Bert looked around again.

Bert: "Well, I think they will start biting now."

He threw his line in and we both started pulling them in. Pretty soon something hit my line and took off with it.

Fred: "Bert, I got a big bass this time."

Bert: "It's a kitty."

I played with the fish awhile and when I got it up to the boat it was a catfish. We fished a little longer and pretty soon Bert pulled in his line and put his gear away and told me that they would not bite anymore today. But I had to fish a little longer to see if he was right. He was! We started home and he passed a couple more motorboats on the way back to the dock.

After Bert got his boat scrubbed down and we got ready to leave I asked him, "How, did you know when the fish were going to start to bite and when they would stop?"

Bert: *"We went out there on the last of the ebb tide but when we got there the tide was still running out too strong to get bottom and so they stopped biting."*

Fred: *"Well, then tell me how you knew that that fish on my line was a catfish before you ever saw it."*

Bert: *"Because it took your line and started out against the tide. Only a foul fish will do that. A fair fish will go with the tide."*

Bert and Lloyd Crichlow were fishing down at Summer Haven one time and on the way back they broke down at Crescent Beach. They were in Bert's rowboat, only now he had a stern-kicker on it. Well, they got up as close to shore as they could and Bert had the kicker in one arm and his gear that he didn't want to leave in the boat in the other arm. Since the bottom was muddy and he had high boots on he told Lloyd to get on his back and he would take him to shore.

Lloyd said, "You're crazy, man. You can't take me too."

Bert said, "Get on my back." So Lloyd got on his back and Bert took him to shore.

Sometime in the 1920s I bought a seventeen-foot canoe and I remember Bert and I went after marsh hens during one northeaster. I handled the paddle and Bert handled the shotgun. We found that canoes were better than rowboats because canoes are lighter draft—you can get them into the marsh sooner because the tide doesn't have to be so high.

Sometimes when the northeaster was real strong and the tide would come over the marsh grass and flush the little baby marsh hens out some of those guys would shoot the babies too small to eat. Sometimes when Bert would see the little ones helpless like that he would go ahead and shoo them back up into higher grass where they could hide. One time he saw a law enforcement officer shooting marsh hens while in a boat with the motor running. That disgusted him to no end. That was against the law as well as poor sportsmanship.

Bert was not a religious person, but he was a good person. He had a good character and he was a true sportsman. He loved the fish and game that he sought and he did not want to see their lives wasted. We need more men like him. He lived close to nature. He and Gertie were devoted to one another and I pray the Lord will find a place in heaven for him.

Bert Hernandez was born October 7, 1899, and died January 14, 1988. He was a businessman, helping his father run Ocean View Hotel, and he served his country driving USO trucks during World War I. For years he earned a living as a house painter, but always maintained his special love of fishing.

The Hernandez name can be traced as far back as 1550 to Diego Hernandez I and his wife Petra. Among the first Florida residents was Jose Hernandez II (born 1745), who married Maria Mier in 1774.

Fisherman's Prayer
By Bert Hernandez

I pray that I may live to fish
Until my dying day
And when it comes to my last cast
I then most humbly pray.
When in the Lord's great landing net
And peacefully I sleep.
That in his mercy I be judged
Big enough to keep.

February 11, 1988

Ocean View has long been replaced by modern motels. The street once called Bay Street was renamed Avenida Menendez along the section described by Pinkham.

BORN IN THE OLDEST WOODEN SCHOOLHOUSE
Cora Maye Large

Cora Maye D. Russell Large was a fascinating woman whose name belies her size. She was a little dynamo who has experienced more unusual feats than most people contemplate. She soloed in a small aircraft, flew in a seaplane, learned to skate while up north, took a John Robert Powers modeling course, did a mean belly dance, was an award-winning swimmer and had always worked with civic and community organizations such as the American Cancer Society and the Girl Scouts. She also has the distinction of having been born in the oldest wooden building in St. Augustine, known as the Oldest Wooden Schoolhouse, seen above.

While living in Clayville, Pennsylvania, Cora Maye was elected to the Borough Council. One of her first assignments was street beautification and she left her male colleagues thunderstruck with her approach. She gathered up all the garbage cans, painted them white and decorated them with flowers and little bees, beetles and butterflies. Cora Maye also wrote poetry, paints and raised championship cocker spaniels. Here are her memories of growing up in St. Augustine, and of working during World War II.

I was born here in St. Augustine in the Oldest Wooden Schoolhouse. Of course it wasn't the Oldest Schoolhouse then. It was my grandmother's shop. My grandmother [Cora May Morris Kearns] had a gift shop there, which she ran every winter. She

had a shop in Wildwood, New Jersey—Kearns Leather Goods. Then in the winter she and my grandfather would come down here to open up because she was a native of St. Augustine. I was born in the back room on Christmas Eve. Dr. Horace Lindsey had to be called out at night. That was the doctor that lived in the big house on St. George Street. My mother was not in the best of health and she and my father were living in the back room so my grandmother could help out.

My grandmother's shop supplied leather goods, souvenirs, pennants and leather items she could burn names in—like a gift shop today. She had chinaberry beads. I used to help her string those. I don't know how she got the little holes in the beads, but she dyed them different colors. She put these little gold beads against the chinaberry bead itself and then would string a gold bead on the other side. Sometimes there would be leather beads we would put in between.

We must have lived there for a while because I have a letter of condolence to my father addressed 14 St. George Street when my mother died. I was born in 1914 and my brother was born in April of 1916. My mother died in October of that year.

When my father got married again we lived in a little house on Hypolita Street, right where Standard Printing is now. I remember it because we used to take our kiddy car, get over the fence, and go over to see my grandmother in this two-story house on Charlotte Street and mother would scold us and grandmother would send us back with a flower so mother wouldn't scold us.

Then we moved to 6 Charlotte Street. That was where my sister Susan was born. Then we moved to 74 Saragossa where two more of my sisters and my brother were born. Then, when the Depression came along, we moved to 14 Rhode. My youngest sister Kathleen was born there. That was when I was in nurse's training up in Philadelphia.

After I left, the family moved to Shenandoah in a house that Mr. Warden built for his daughter when she was married. It was a beautiful home, but now it's a filling station. My father sold it when they moved out to May Street.

It really was a lovely home. It had a front stairway and a back stairway and the windows were from the floor to the ceiling. It had fireplaces, a large living room, large dining room and sort of like a little porch my father used for an office. Then you went into a breakfast room and the back stairs went up from there. There was a large kitchen.

I lived in that house with my family while my husband Fred went to war. Fred left for overseas in March 1943 and I came here in the summer after trying to enter the air force. I worked at Flagler Hospital during '43, '44 and '45. I spent six months on night duty. Mrs. Francis Small was the nursing supervisor at the time. There was a joke around the hospital about us. She was so large and her name was Mrs. Small. I was so small and I was Mrs. Large. Everyone thought that was so funny.

Flood waters from the 1944 hurricane pushed Usina's dock across Bay Street up to the Elks Lodge front door.

My sister Isabelle worked at Flagler too. She and Tommy Thompson and I used to walk home together. We would walk along the seawall, eyes glued to the ground looking for money that the soldiers would drop. I don't know how they could lose so much money, but they did. There were always coins all along the seawall.

There were men everywhere then. The fliers from Green Cove on R&R [rest and recuperation] and fliers from Cecil Field, the coast guard from Daytona and those stationed at Ponce de Leon [Hotel], then the military from Blanding. Some slept in the park or hotel lobbies. There wasn't enough room.

My sisters dated fliers and at times we all went out as a group. I had three eligible sisters and one about seven years old. I was married but we would all go to the beach or to the movies.

Work at the hospital was sometimes difficult. We worked from seven in the evening until seven in the morning with a little time off to sleep on the porch. All the patients were housed on the second floor. The north end was all private and semi-private rooms. This was when penicillin first came in. It was given in the muscle with a large hypodermic needle. It was a large dose of liquid. I felt sorry for the people to whom I gave it.

In the fall of 1944 a good-sized hurricane hit. I was working that night. We had no electricity—no lights or call bells. We used candles and flashlights. The water came up to the back of the hospital. When it was time for us to go home we had to walk through waist-deep water. Wires were down across the streets. We had to detour via South Street and I think Cordova. Part of the seawall broke through in the morning and there were great waves across Bay Street.

When I got home my mother saw me coming into the yard. She yelled from the porch as I pushed open the picket fence gate. "Close the gate quick. Don't let the water get in."

[Cora Maye laughed in delight at that last comment and then ended her tale.]

In 1945 I went back north to join my husband. But that's another story entirely.

The "Oldest Wooden Schoolhouse" is a one-and-a-half-story frame building constructed around 1800–1810 and is the oldest wooden structure in St. Augustine. The building was long associated with the Genopoly family from the time of purchase of the vacant lot in 1778 by Juan Genopoly to the final property exchange in 1904 by Genopoly's grandson, John J. Darling. Darling bequeathed the property to his neighbors Eunice and Frank Greatroex, who leased the property for commercial use. It was at this time that Thomas and Cora Kearns operated a novelty shop in the building, promoting the structure by advertising their business as being in the oldest frame house in St. Augustine. They were also the first to call it "the Old, Old, Schoolhouse," although there has never been evidence of use in that capacity. A picture of Cora Maye Large hangs in the room where she was born.

The hurricane that Cora Maye remembers occurred in October 1944. A *Record* headline on October 18 proclaims the news "Hurricane Nears Florida," and proceeds to describe the damage inflicted on Havana, Cuba, by 160-mile-per-hour winds. The next day an abbreviated front page of the *Record* quietly reports that "at 4:38 p.m. AP wire informed the *Record* that the hurricane had passed the city at 3:00 p.m. traveling to sea at 60 miles per hour. Not within the memory of the oldest citizens of St. Augustine has a storm wrought such havoc in the Ancient City as today's."

An article the following day informs readers that the city was drying out and describes water damage from floods up to twelve inches deep in the house on Bay Street. The 1944 hurricane is certainly a lasting memory for all those who experienced the storm as Cora Maye did.

April 7, 1988

Standard Printing is no longer at the Avilles Street location. The stretch of Bay Street between Castillo de San Marcos to St. Francis Barracks has been renamed Avenida Menendez.

REMEMBERING MARJORIE
Norton Baskin (Part I)

Norton Baskin was born in Alabama where he lived until he was seventeen. After a six-year stay in Atlanta, Georgia, he traveled to Florida where he worked in various capacities including newspaper columnist. After a second short stay in Georgia, this time Valdosta, Mr. Baskin moved to Ocala to manage a hotel. He married famed author Marjorie Kinnan Rawlings, seen in the above photograph sitting at her typewriter in her Cross Creek home. Here is the rest of the story.

Cross Creek was autobiographical but nine out of ten stories in there—you know she had any number of stories and characters in there—had an O'Henry ending. I mean it was fictional to that extent. They were real people and these things happened, but the catch line was what made it.

Then when you come to the movie, well, there were some fifty-seven characters in Cross Creek. They couldn't have all of them, so they combined them. For instance Geechee was a combination of about five different people. Marjorie had hundreds of maids. Martha was the main one. In the movie, Geechee comes and says she has come to take up the slack—well that was old Martha. She and her husband Will came and moved into the servants' house—the old slave quarters—and every time Marjorie would get a maid or would need someone, well right then Martha would have a daughter who was free to come. There were four of those that came and that didn't include Kate or Geechee or anyone else.

The story that Marjorie told about Geechee was true—up to a point. For instance, Geechee did leave with that terrible husband. Then later on Marjorie fell and broke her neck and she went to Leesburg to find Geechee. She broke her neck right when she was in the middle of writing Golden Apples. *What happened was that she was on a horse. She wanted to go to the right and the horse wanted to go to the left—and both of them did. She fell off and literally broke her neck. But she had to finish* Golden Apples. *There was a deadline because* Cosmopolitan *was serializing it and they had already printed two chapters and she was still working on the ending. She had to finish it with a neck brace on. And she had to go down to Leesburg to find Geechee—the real Geechee. She was in a gyp joint where she was plying a trade and drinking whiskey. And that's when the character Geechee came about. You know that scene where Geechee says, "You let me go..." Well, she really said, "You let me go away with him," but Marjorie took her back. She took care of Marjorie while she had that thing on.*

But Geechee was so much on the bottle herself she came and told Marjorie, "This ain't gonna work out. I can't stay here this way." She left again. That's why the picture Cross Creek *is different from life. Those things happened, but with a slightly different ending.*

You asked me about me. No, that's not the way I met Marjorie. Of course Marjorie came down there. She came in '28 with her husband—her husband then—and his two brothers. The three of them stayed out there at Cross Creek. I didn't come down until 1933. And, no, she didn't drive herself down from New York alone like in the movie. Probably the brothers drove.

In the movie Cross Creek *they said their goodbyes in New York. That wasn't true. They lived in Cross Creek together until 1932. The two brothers left and Marjorie and Chuck Rawlings stayed there. They both had been newspaper people. Marjorie had been with Hurst newspapers where she learned the ins and outs of that kind of journalism. But she always wanted to do fiction. I think her mother died and she got this inheritance and with that she came down and bought seventy-seven acres of orange groves. Chuck was not happy there a'tall. He got along fine for awhile. He was with the moonshiners making whiskey and everything like that—living the life that she writes about. His main journalistic thing, though, was on boating and yachts and racing and things to do with that. He went over to the East Coast to Tarpon Springs and wrote there. Then he got to going back to New York where he was fairly successful. He was going back and forth between Cross Creek and New York, but then one last time they both decided that was it. Supposedly it was a very amicable parting. They both knew this was the end. Marjorie never told me any of it. She never talked about him at*

The author's home is now part of the Marjorie Kinnan Rawlings Historic State Park.
Photo by Matt McCarthy

all. She wanted a clean break. I think he tried to come back a couple of times, but she wouldn't have that. I think he understood.

But then, as far as Marjorie meeting me at the hotel...I was a hotel man but, gracious, I had 157 elegant rooms in Ocala so I wouldn't have known her when she walked up.

Although, I have to admit later I was amazed that I hadn't heard of her. All my life I've been a reader. It's all I ever wanted to do. So when I went down to Ocala I should have known who she was. But her first good book, at least the first one that got any recognition, came out just a month before I went to Ocala. That was South Moon Under. *Of course it was taken by the Book-of-the-Month Club and became quite the thing.*

I went down to Ocala from Valdosta, Georgia, to manage a hotel. It was one of those home-owned by the townspeople hotels. It was built with their money and they had to take it over. They had had nineteen managers in two years' time because so many people had to be pleased. I knew I had to do something to get on their good side.

The day I arrived to take over I realized that all these people owned it and I had to make friends with them. I looked on the calendar and, on the third day after I arrived, the St. Agnes Guild from the Episcopal Church was holding their yearly fundraising party at the hotel. There was a lady named Dorothy Green who was in charge. She got in touch with me and asked me to come in to talk. I promised her I would have everything set up. So, the night of the event, I realized these are the people I've go to know and impress. So when they came in I was standing there greeting everybody. Then when they all got in there—there were forty tables, that's 160 people—I went in there with a pushcart and bellboy's uniform and ice water and glasses and went all around. I would introduce myself and pour water for everyone. Well, she thought that was wonderful and the thing went over beautifully.

About three days later Dorothy Green called me up and said, "Listen, you are new in town. What are you doing tonight?"

I said, "Nothing in particular. Why?"

She said, "How about going out to Cross Creek with us?"

"Where the h—— is Cross Creek?" I asked.

"It's about fourteen miles from here, but it's where Marjorie Rawlings lives."

"Who the h—— is Marjorie Rawlings?" I asked.

"Well, potentially she's as good a writer as you're ever going to know in your life. She's just had this book published. It's with the Book-of-the-Month Club. Come on out with us. She's just putting in for a divorce. My husband is her lawyer and we think she needs some cheering up."

Five of them were going out so I said, "Sure," and I went with them. When we drove up, the others all knew her and they greeted and greeted and Dorothy said, "Marjorie, this is Norton Baskin."

She didn't know I was coming because she didn't have a telephone. But she said, "Norton Baskin?"

I said, "Yes."

"Oh," she said. "I've been wanting to meet you."

"What in the world for? How do you know me?"

"You are the new manager of the hotel?" she asked.

I said yes and she told me to come inside. She had this newspaper clipping she read to me. It said the St. Agnes Guild had this bridge party at the hotel. "During the evening," it proclaimed, "Mr. Baskin, the new manager of the hotel, had passed water at every table."

Marjorie said, "I wanted to see the man who could do that!"

On that bawdy note we became very good friends.

Now years later, Marjorie and I knew we were going to be married but we couldn't set a date because my way of life is so different from hers. I'm this gregarious hotel man whose whole life depended on people—on being around them and entertaining them. She was practically a hermit. She didn't dislike people, but she didn't like them in the mass. Cross Creek was perfect for her because she hated cities. She had her friends out there and she turned her back on so many other types of people. She didn't like the middle ground, and those were the folks I knew. She thought the real Crackers were really somebody that could get a living out of anything. She didn't think they were lawbreakers or immoral. She thought this was the way they had to live.

We knew we were going to be married, but she knew she couldn't come and live in a hotel and be a hotel man's wife. She wanted me to give it up but I was just getting to where I was making some money. So we thought it was time for me to have my own hotel. There wasn't anything in Ocala so I contacted Verle Pope in St. Augustine. The first thing he did was show me Flagler's home, Kirkside. But it was off the beaten path and wouldn't do.

Then Verle called me and told me Mr. [Walter B.] Fraser had something he wanted to talk to me about. So I went up and he took me to the Alcazar hotel. The hotel had been closed for eighteen years but it was beautiful. The wallpaper looked like it had been hung the day before. But I said, "This is completely out of my territory. I couldn't do a thing like this." The plumbing, electricity and the heating were absolutely gone. To replace that was ten times more than what I could afford.

Then Verle took me up to see the Castle Warden. It also had been vacant for eighteen years. I was fascinated. I met with the Ketterlinus representatives who were as careful about who they were selling to as I was about buying.

I think I paid $18,000 for it. But then I had to borrow some $65,000 to put it in shape. But that was a labor of love.

I brought up a Cracker from Cross Creek whose name was Leonard Fiddeay and was a self-taught builder. We hired locals to build but he was the supervisor. I knew about Lizzie Ketterlinus, who had owned the place, because everyone told me what I could or couldn't do because of Lizzie. Well, we started working up on the third floor. In the back room there was a dressmaker's life-size frame of Lizzie. Somebody had put a hat on her and draped the craziest-looking fur around her. Each time the workers finished a room they moved Lizzie with them. She always went with them. When they moved down to the second floor, Lizzie went with them. When they moved down to the first floor, Lizzie went with them. The first time I went up to Castle Warden and found Lizzie on the front porch, I knew we were through.

I had any number of sidewalk superintendents: Dr. Britt, Dr. White and Judge Jackson. All of them had something to say—and all of them were dear friends of Lizzie.

Marjorie and I got married just before I opened the hotel. It was October 1941. Shortly after, we had a grand open house that Verle Pope helped me with. He introduced me as we greeted the guests and then we sent them up to Marjorie. It was a good party.

I kept the hotel until 1946, when I sold it. Marjorie and I had a house on the beach then and we were very happy together.

Marjorie Kinnan Rawlings is one of Florida's best-known authors. Her books about Florida include *South Moon Under*, *Cross Creek*, *Cross Creek Cookery*, *When the Whippoorwill* and *Golden Apples*. Her book *The Yearling* won the Pulitzer Prize in 1939 and was made into a movie of the same name.

Marjorie was born in Washington, D.C., in 1896 and moved to her Florida orange grove at age twenty-eight. Her love for the Florida countryside is reflected in her many publications.

The Castle Warden, purchased by Norton Baskin and renovated as a hotel, stands at 19 San Marco Avenue and currently serves as Ripley's Believe it or Not!® Museum. The Moorish Revival structure was completed in 1879 as the home for millionaire William G. Warden and his large family. The last resident was a Warden daughter, Elizabeth B. Ketterlinus, the "Lizzie" in Baskin's story.

Ketterlinus High School, now a middle school, was named for Mrs. Ketterlinus, who was very fond of St. Augustine. Verle Pope, mentioned in the story, served in the state legislature for twenty-four years and was known as the "Lion of the Senate." A native of St. Augustine, he died here in 1973.

May 19, 1988

Originally a high school, the educational institution bearing the Ketterlinus name has been transformed numerous times over the years, now serving the kindergarten and elementary grade levels.

Flagler's mansion, Kirkside, was demoslished in 1950 and replaced by residences and an apartment building.

Courtesy of Sara Hooker and the Norton Baskin family

FILMING
CROSS CREEK
Norton Baskin (Part II)

In a previous interview, Norton Baskin talked of meeting and marrying Florida author Marjorie Kinnan Rawlings. He spoke about his work as a hotel man and related how he purchased Castle Warden here in St. Augustine, converting it into a hotel in 1941. This tale opens with a response to the question, "What did you think of the movie *Cross Creek?*" Baskin was on location for part of the filming and is seen above with Mary Steenburgen, who played Marjorie, and Peter Coyote, who played Mr. Baskin.

I'm prejudiced of course but I thought it was a beautiful thing. I thought it was very well done. And I thought Mary Steenburgen did a beautiful job. In fact, Mary and I got along just fine. I was there [on location] *for the filming any number of times. They asked me to come and work with Mary and Peter* [Coyote] *and Rip Torn. Mary wanted to find out all she could about Marjorie and we got to know each other well. As a matter of fact, Mary and I swore undying love.*

Also, the film people would have me come over and talk to them about things. I was over there for four days once and had just come home when the phone rang and it was the boss, Mr. Radnitz, saying they wanted me to come and be in the movie. But I said, "Hell, I am the movie. Who do you think Peter's playing?"

But he said he didn't want me to act—that was the last thing he wanted. But then he said they had seen me on some TV things I had done and I looked fine. So I agreed to go on up there.

Well, I got there and checked into a suite of rooms they had gotten me. They told me they were sending a girl over with some papers to sign and they would expect me at seven o'clock the next morning. Someone would pick me up and take me to the set where they were filming. Then they gave me the script and I had just one line to say so I figured, I can say that.

The girl came back later with my contract and I asked her what that was all about. She said that I had to sign it, and I had to join the Screen Actors Guild. It had all these details about how many hours I could work during a day and for how many days. I argued that I only had one line and didn't need all of that. But she said you never know how these things go.

They picked me up the next morning. Peter was with me and so was the little girl. They took me to my dressing room and told me first they would come around with my costume and then they would bring accessories. After that I would go to makeup. Well, I thought the makeup idea was just fine—I would come out looking like Clark Gable or Cary Grant and this was going to be very nice.

My costume was already laid out in the dressing room so I got into that. Then someone came around and took my ring and my watch off. They said the watch was too modern and the ring had to go because it had my initials on it and I was not Norton Baskin in the movie. They gave me a pocket watch fob and everything. Then a man came to check my hair. That was all right because I was going to have a hat on. Then finally they came to take me to makeup.

I went in and there was a little East Indian girl who was doing the makeup. She pushed me a little this way and a little that way and put my hat on. Then she said she was going to put a little powder on to hide my sun tan. Well, she did that and said that was it.

I said, "Is that all? I thought you were going to make me look like something."

She said, "Mr. Baskin, it says here you are playing a little old man. You are a little old man."

And that was all the makeup they gave me.

In the scene, I was to be sitting in a rocker in front of the little grocery store. Mary's car breaks down and she comes along and says to me, "Please, I need help. I need a taxi. Can you direct me to a taxi?"

I say, "There are no taxis. You need the hotel. Just go over to the hotel and ask for Norton Baskin. He'll take care of you." They forgot to tell me where the hotel was. So, when she came up from that way, I realized it had to be the other way, so I pointed in the opposite direction from where she came. The director said that was

Workers in the 1940s transformed Castle Warden into a hotel for Norton Baskin. *Courtesy of Norton Baskin*

just fine, but I wasn't supposed to see Mary. I was supposed to act surprised. So we tried it again.

The next time around somebody moved in the scene and ruined it. Anyway, it took eight solid hours to do that one scene. One time the director said again I was doing fine, but he said, "when you say, 'Ask for Norton Baskin. He'll take care of you,' you should make it sound like Norton can do anything."

"Well," I said. "That was easy. He could."

You want a story about Peter? In Hollywood Peter went to try out for the part of the Cracker father of the little girl. They told him they had already given the part to Rip Torn, but they said he could read for the part of Norton Baskin. He didn't know anything about Norton Baskin except he was Marjorie's husband. He got the part and they handed him the script to study and told him to be ready in three weeks. But he didn't know anything about me. All the script said was that Baskin was a snappy dresser and loved women. So Peter went to the library and tried to get any information he could. He found out about a man who had written about Marjorie and he tried to get hold of him to learn more about me. But the man wouldn't agree to talk to him unless he was hired as a consultant and paid a fee. Peter begged him and explained he just wanted to learn more about Baskin. Finally Peter said, "You're my only chance to find out about this man. I need to know what he was like."

The man responded, "Why don't you get in touch with him yourself?"

Peter said, "My gosh! Is that old man still alive?"

Then he called me up and asked if he could come see me. Well, Peter got here at 9:00 a.m. one morning. He turned on the tape recorder and stayed all day; then he spent the night. He never turned off the tape recorder. We got up the next morning and he turned it back on. He kept that thing going the entire time. Then when he was ready to go he asked me how I wanted him to play me. I said they were playing me too much like a Cracker. I was an Alabama Cracker, but not one of them—I was never a Florida Cracker. Also, they were playing me rather ignorant.

So Peter said he wasn't planning to play me the least bit ignorant, but how would I like to be played?

"With charm," I said. "With charm." And that's exactly what he did.

The climax of it all was when they asked me to join them in Cannes, where they were showing the movie at the film festival that year. I was able to fly over with some friends from here. I was feeling kind of bad from jet lag when I first got there, but Mr. Radnitz said they wanted me to come to a press conference the next day and that Mary and Peter would be there. So the next morning they picked me up and took me to this beautiful place where everyone was gathering. Mr. Radnitz greeted me and asked me if I had seen Mary yet. I said no, and he told me she was right around the corner. So I went to find her. I saw her standing with her husband, Malcolm McDonald, with her back turned toward me. Well, it had been a year and a half since I had seen her. I walked up behind her and said, "Hello, Mary."

Well, she turned around and there she was, very beautiful—but seven months' pregnant.

I shook my head and turned to McDonald and said, "What have you been doing with my wife!"

We all laughed and had a good time about that. The film never won any awards but a major studio, Universal I believe, picked it up and, well, I guess you could say it's been popular ever since.

Cross Creek, filmed in 1982, has been played on cable TV and is available on videocassette. It was directed by Robert B. Radnitz and produced by Martin Ritt. Dana Hill played the young girl, Ellen.

Readers interested in visiting The Marjorie Kinnan Rawling's State Historic site should be cautioned that there are restrictions to the number touring the building due to size and age constraints of the structure. It is advised to write or phone in advance for hours of operation and group scheduling.

In recent months an unknown manuscript written by Marjorie Rawlings was discovered. The document was autobiographical and contained family chronicles typed in 1929. The script had been rejected by *Atlantic Monthly* magazine, but now may be edited and published by an English professor with expertise in Southern writing, who is in possession of the papers.

May 26, 1988

Rangers at the Marjorie Kinnan Rawlings site report a recent renewed interest in the author and her Florida country life.

TURPENTINE INDUSTRY
Elliott Maguire

Elliott Maguire was born into the turpentine business. His mother's father, Elliott Erastus Edge, was a native of the naval stores region of North Carolina who migrated to Florida with his turpentining knowledge and his wife Cornelia Paterson. Elliott's father, Leo Maguire, went into business with E.E. Edge in 1925 and bought Edge's interest in the business after Edge died.

The current Maguire Timber Corporation can be traced back to 1893, with a progression of businesses including Edge Mercantile, Edge Realty, Maguire Timber, Maguire Land and Maguire and Lewis.

Elliott has a sister, Joan Lewis, and a brother Robert (Bob). When Leo took sons Elliott and Bob into the business, the name became Maguire Timber Company. After the Vietnam War, Elliott's son Craig began buying interests in the company, which soon became Maguire Timber Corporation. Members of the Maguire family remain active in community planning through participation on the board of county commissioners.

This is Elliott Maguire's story about the community of Elwood and the turpentine business.

Elwood's history goes back to the turpentine business. Time was when the turpentine business and naval stores was one of the best businesses in North Florida. It was

almost as large as the cotton business after the Civil War. [The term "naval stores" refers to the fact that products were used for caulking and rigging on wooden ships.]

Elwood was formed by my daddy as a turpentine camp. He called it Elwood after his hometown of Elwood, Indiana. He had tried to make a name out of the first two initials of my name and my brother Bob's and sister Joan's names. But Elbojo, Joelbo or Bojoel didn't work. But Elwood made sense. The "wood" is appropriate.

Let me tell you a little about the turpentine business before we talk about Elwood. The naval stores part of the turpentine business really goes back to the Bible. God commanded Noah to build an ark and to make it safe within and without with pitch and tar. Pitch and tar were the forerunners of turpentine and rosin.

A lot of the history goes back to the British. The British sailors were called Tars—Jack-tars. They got the name because they would use this pitch and tar to caulk the seams of the ships. It was dirty work, so it was used as punishment. It was especially bad on the main deck. They called it paying instead of caulking. They would have to pay the seams and then if they walked on the tar it would be gummy and sticky and make a mess on the deck. Then they would have to take sandstone and clean the deck.

As I say, it was used for punishment because the men wouldn't want to do it and they had to do that on their off hours. The worst place was the longest seam down the main deck, and that was called the devil. So they had to "pay the devil." That's how the saying got started of "You have to pay the devil," or the "devil to pay."

The sailors weren't ones to be too clean back in those days. They started putting tar on their hair. Back then so many men, sailors in particular, wore their hair braided up into a ponytail. During the week or when they were at sea they didn't do much to it. But then when they got into port for liberty they would put tar on their hair.

They didn't change shirts very often and they didn't want to get tar on them. They would put a big cloth collar around their uniform so the tar would get on that. Then instead of washing their shirt they would simply wash the big collar. And, you see, that is still part of the sailor's uniform.

Then, after the Civil War, people in the business started improving on the system of how to get the pitch and how to get the rosin and, eventually, how to make the turpentine. As they started doing that, they found out the states farther south—South Carolina, Georgia and Florida—had better trees.

They learned how to put streaks on the trees. They would take something like a knife and pull across the tree and cut through the bark and the cambium layer to the wood. Then gum comes out and down the face of the tree and catches in a cup. Then it is collected and brought to the camp in barrels where it is stilled.

At one time you could hardly drive through north Florida or south Georgia

Joe and Carriebell Smiley stand with their granddaughter, Felicia, in front of the last extant structure moved from Old Julia. For a time, Joe ran a store in the building. The Smiley's son, Anthony, excelled at football at St. Augustine High School and Florida State University. *Photo by Karen Harvey*

without being able to see turpentine trees—same way over into Alabama, Mississippi and Louisiana.

The streaking stunted their growth some, but it didn't harm them. The growth of the trees is in the cambium layer just below the bark. Now, if you cut the cambium layer all around the tree, then you would kill it. The streaked part was called a turpentine face. When the face was low they would work it with a hack. When the face got higher they used a puller. The face could be streaked about a foot and a half a year and could go up to about ten feet. The gum would be accumulated, put in the barrels and brought to the still. Daddy had a still made of copper, which held seven barrels of gum. It was surrounded by brick to insulate it. They would put a copper cap over the kettle part of it, which went over to a worm—a copper pipe about four inches in diameter. It circled down through a wooden tank that had water in it for cooling. Steam would come up from the water being boiled in the drum. It would capture the steam, put it back down through the copper tube called the worm, and go inside the tank, which was about six or eight feet tall. The gum was poured into the tank at the second-floor level. In the late 1930s there must have been a half dozen or a dozen stills in St. Johns County.

Water would cool the steam and condense it. Then, when it came out the bottom, you had water and spirits of turpentine. Water would go to the bottom, and the spirits of turpentine would go to the top. They would siphon that off into oak wooden barrels. That was what brought the best price. Then what was left in the kettle was poured out into a vat and strained through three different strainers to get all the impurities out—impurities meaning bark, wood chips, anything of that type.

Most turpentine operations had their own cooper shop. A cooper was a man who made the barrels for the rosin. The rosin did not have to be as good as the turpentine. You would get barrel staves made up in a bundle and the cooper would make the barrel. When it cooled, it would harden. Then they would put a top on it and ship it to wherever.

Much of the turpentine was exported. Savannah once was the biggest center for turpentine and rosin in the world and Jacksonville got almost that big. Once it was such a big industry in the South, but now it is almost all gone. What happened was it was labor intensive—and cheap labor. When World War II came along it was already a dying industry because of the cost of labor. Then the pulp mills came in and they made the same products as by-products.

The way I got into the business was like this. My granddad and my grandmother on my mother's side were born and raised in North Carolina. She was raised in Jackson Springs and he was raised south of Fayetteville. His name was Elliott Erastus Edge. My name is Elliott, and I've always been glad they didn't name me Erastus. My grandparents were married in North Carolina and then moved down into Georgia. Incidentally, when they were married my grandmother was thirteen years old. When the first baby was born she was fifteen years old. They got off to an early start.

My grandfather had been working for other people [in the turpentine business] up until the time they moved to Georgia. Once he was there he started in the turpentine business on his own. They didn't live in Georgia very long. They moved on down into Lake County, Florida, and settled in Groveland south of Leesburg.

We say our business started when Granddad went into business for himself in 1893. He formed Edge Mercantile Company at that time. The companies would build their own houses for all their employees. They were board-and-batten and were actually more shanties than houses. They always called it a turpentine camp. I don't know why they called it a camp because it was permanent, but they did. They had a company store, which they called a commissary. Also, there usually was one building that would serve as the church on Sunday and the schoolhouse during the week.

While my granddaddy and grandmother lived in Groveland, he owned a turpentine business and a sawmill. Then they got into planting citrus. The orange business started up around Mandarin and Fish Island, but freezes caused it to move farther south. So around 1900 they started planting citrus in Lake County. The family still has some groves around there.

Edge had two daughters and one son and my dad married one of his daughters. My dad was born in Indiana and worked in a steel mill. His dad's health was real bad and they recommended that he move to Florida. So he settled around Groveland, where he met my mother.

My dad was a teenage boy, I guess, when they first moved down. When Mother and Daddy married they moved back to Indiana and he worked in a steel mill a little while. That's where I was born. Then eventually my granddad Edge took my daddy into business. They formed Edge Mercantile and Realty. Then they spun part of the business off and started Edge and Maguire Turpentine. My granddad Edge was a great one to put up some capital and be a silent partner. Anyway, my dad and mother went into the turpentine business with my granddad down in Myakka City in Manatee County. When they worked out all the timber, they closed down the operation and bought what they called Old Julia, a turpentine operation close to Orangedale.

Back then most of the turpentine operations were financed by what they called a factorage house. The one my dad dealt with was T&R Turpentine and Rosin Factors. The person doing the factoring would give you an account that you could draw against. Turpentine generally was made in the summer so it was a yearly thing, and a continuing thing. You'd borrow enough money to take you through the year, and at the end of the year they'd hold a settlement and get approval to finance through the next year. This was going on all over the South—Georgia, north Florida and right on into what corresponds to the Cotton Belt, the Bible Belt and the Black (soil) Belt. Turpentine operations were all over those areas.

If a turpentine operator like the one that owed Old Julia wanted to get out of business, then he would tell the factorage house and, hopefully, they would know someone who wanted to buy a turpentine operation. That's how my dad bought Old Julia.

The deed for Old Julia goes back to 1928. It shows he bought twenty-one shanties, two dwellings, mules, horses, tools and the commissary—all that. It says also, "All hands' accounts" referring to the money the employees owned to the company store. Then there is the item on the deed that says, "1 (one) still and fixtures, together with lease on still thermometer."

It used to be that the man who made the turpentine rosin was considered skilled labor because he had to get it to the right temperature and keep it there for however long. They didn't have thermometers to speak of at that time. Down at the bottom of the worm, he could put his ear up to a certain place and hear the gum boiling in the kettle. A skilled man could tell by the sound of the gum boiling how it was doing.

Then they got around to using a thermometer. They must have been expensive because the deed shows they leased it instead of buying it. I remember the one Daddy had was about a foot and a half tall. You just don't see many thermometers a foot and a half tall. They moved the turpentine operation here from Myakka City in 1928. It was a major operation. It was about 225 miles. They had two Model-T trucks for moving. I believe it was twenty-one families, horses, mules, at least one cow, chickens, dogs, employees and families. Not all the roads were paved.

Then around 1937, Daddy decided to move the operation to Elwood. It wasn't called anything at the time. He just bought a piece of land. You lease turpentine trees from landowners, and you want your operation to be in the middle of all those leases. They moved about twenty houses, but they didn't move the old commissary. They built this commissary [in Elwood], *and the building used as a church and school.*

In 1943 Daddy sold almost all his land [ten thousand acres]. *The turpentine business was on its way out. In the meantime he was getting into the pulp wood business, so it was just kind of a transition. We kept the commissary for a while, but we actually didn't need it.*

The employees were all blacks. The overseer was called a woods rider and would go around checking on the men. Each man would have a crop of about ten thousand faces. The idea was to try to get a streak not more than two weeks apart. A man had to be in good physical shape to do it. I think that seven or eight thousand was more realistic for putting a streak on every two weeks. The man putting the streak on worked alone and the woods rider would ride around and check. They were paid per streak, so the more ambitious workers earned the most.

Then there were dip squads to get the gum out. Since dipping was done in the summertime, a lot of the ones doing the dipping were the older boys. A man would drive the dip wagon and each boy would go out and fill the bucket. When the bucket got full he'd go back and take it to the dip wagon. The driver would record how many buckets each dipper brought in, and they would get paid for that. Most of the workers stayed on and just changed jobs. Many of the people who live in Elwood were born out there and are descendants of the Myakka City employees. Some are second or third generations of the original employees. The names are Bennett, Raggins, Johnson, Smiley, Joe Lewis Frazer, James Jones, Andrew Johnson and Andrew Johnson Jr.

We don't have many employees in the business now because we sub-contract the work. But we see the folks often and know how they are doing.

According to Stanley C. Bond Jr., archaeologist at the Historic St. Augustine Preservation Board, turpentine camps were given letter designations, probably related to the grade of turpentine. A name was derived from the letter; thus "Julia" most likely came from the camp letter "J."

Bond noted that the "naval stores industry had a major impact on the economy and settlement of St. Johns County." Naval stores production is documented as early as the seventeenth century, but the British were the first to make it extensive and profitable.

Bond's paper, "The Development of the Naval Stores Industry in St. Johns County, Florida" and other research is available at the St. Augustine Historical Society.

April 26, 1990

Although the commissary is crumbling, it is still visible alongside the streets of modest, neat homes inhabited by families about whom Maguire spoke.

Courtesy of Mrs. Noble Putnam Calhoun

RICH LINEAGE EXPLORED
Noble Putnam Calhoun

Noble Putnam Calhoun has more than just an aristocratic-sounding name. He has a lineage that includes a United States vice-president, a Confederate general, judges, lawyers, doctors and an admiral. His St. Augustine connections include Judge Joseph Lee Smith, the first judge of the Supreme Court for East Florida, and Judge Benjamin Alexander Putnam, for whom the adjoining county is named.

Put's father was born in New York, but told Put that was only "because my mother was there"; he was a lifelong resident of St. Augustine. Through his maternal grandmother, Gertrude de Medici MacWilliams, he can trace his lineage to the Minorcan settlers of the British Period (1763–84). He is seen in the photo above (center) with his sister Gertrude Calhoun (Mrs. Milton E. Bacon) and South Carolina Governor Richard Riley. In 1979 the Calhoun family presented this portrait of their esteemed ancestor John C. Calhoun to the state of South Carolina.

First we'll discuss my lineage as far as Benjamin Alexander Putnam is concerned. It should be noted that Putnam County is named for him and he was prominent in St. Augustine for several reasons. He was speaker of the House of Representatives in Tallahassee at one time. He was also mayor of St. Augustine, and was a colonel during the Seminole Indian wars.

We're talking about way back in the early and middle nineteenth century. His home, where he was reared, was right where the current Lyon Building is [King and St. George Streets]. *My grandfather, Benjamin Alexander Putnam Calhoun, was born there in 1855, although the Calhoun family members were reared mainly in Palatka.*

Judge Putnam married Helen Kirby. This is where the Kirby-Smith family comes in. The Smiths and the Kirbys were both from Litchfield, Connecticut, and they migrated down to St. Augustine in the early nineteenth century. Joseph L. Smith began practicing law with Judge Putnam down here and that's where the connection comes in. Well, he married Helen and they had one daughter whose name was Kate Putnam. My youngest daughter is named for her.

Kate Putnam's first marriage was to John C. Calhoun Jr., who was a doctor. They had two children, John C. Calhoun and Benjamin Alexander Putnam Calhoun, who was my grandfather. When Kate's husband died prematurely she turned around and married his younger brother, William Lowndes Calhoun. They had another son named William Lowndes Calhoun [Jr.], *so they were half brothers and double first cousins.*

That's where the lineage of the Calhoun family comes in from the Kirby-Smiths. Now my grandfather, Benjamin Alexander Putnam Calhoun, was General Kirby-Smith's second cousin. General Kirby-Smith was a very interesting man. He was the only Confederate general who never surrendered. He was in command of the trans-Mississippi department in Shreveport, Louisiana. After the war was over he became chancellor of what was then called the University of the South, now Sewanee, up in the mountains of Tennessee. General Kirby-Smith was the first child christened at the Trinity Episcopal Church in St. Augustine. He was born in the house on Aviles Street that is the old public library.

By the way, let me tell you where I was born. I was born right across the street from the Record *company* [St. Augustine Record *on Cordova Street*] *in the three-story white house two houses down from the synagogue. My grandfather, my mother's father, W.A. MacWilliams, owned that house. He was president of the Florida state Senate back in the '20s and served as a state senator for many, many years. He also was adjutant general of the state of Florida and served in the Spanish American War. That's why they call him General MacWilliams.*

There was intermarriage with the Putnam and Calhoun families, as well as with the Kirby-Smiths. Kate Kirby Putnam married John C. Calhoun Jr. and that's where my grandfather comes in. Patrick Calhoun migrated to this country from Donegal County, Ireland. He first settled in Pennsylvania, then migrated to Virginia, and finally to the Long Canes settlement, which became the Abbeville district of South Carolina. They were farmers.

"Put" Calhoun's ancestry includes the Kirby-Smith family. Pictured here is Frances Kirby, the wife of Judge Joseph Lee Smith and mother of Confederate General Edmund Kirby-Smith. Frances and her sister Helen Putnam were known Confederates spies.

He had several children, one of whom happened to be John C. Calhoun, my great-great-grandfather. His son was John C. Calhoun Jr., who married Kate Putnam. They had two boys, one of whom was my grandfather who was named for Judge Putnam, Benjamin Alexander Putnam Calhoun. Then there was my father, Edward Noble Calhoun. The Noble name was a very prominent name in the Calhoun family. Most of them were attorneys at law. All three of my names are family names.

A little-known fact about Calhoun is that he was selected by John F. Kennedy as one of the five outstanding United States senators of all times. Kennedy was chairman of a committee that was appointed by the Senate to name the men. There was Clay, Webster and Calhoun—they were the triumvirate, you remember. Then there were two others whom I don't recall at this moment.

Anyway, Calhoun got into politics after he graduated from Yale University. He started practicing law in Abbeville, South Carolina. Then he was encouraged by friends to run for a seat in Congress in the House of Representatives, which he did. He spent a total of forty-two years in public life in one capacity or another. He served as a member of Congress, a member of the Senate twice and as vice-president of the United States for two terms. He also was secretary of war during the War of 1812. He was one of what they called the "young hawks" back in those days. He was instrumental in getting the U.S. into war against England.

Calhoun also served as secretary of state. He was recognized as the foremost orator of his day and was considered a brilliant man. I have in my library complete first additions of the first bill of nullification, his philosophy of secession and everything he stood for.

I remember going to Washington as a child. We went into the Senate chambers and my father said, "I want you to sit in that chair." I guess I was nine or ten at the time and I asked why. He said, "Because your great-great-grandfather sat in that chair." I couldn't have cared less who sat in that chair. But, you know, the older you get the more interested you are in the heritage you have.

A lot of people are curious about why Calhoun never became president of the United States. I can tell you why. His wife was from Charleston and was very much a socialite and aristocrat. She was the leader of Washington society during the time Andrew Jackson was president of the United States and Calhoun was his vice-president. It was during this time that a lady by the name of Peggy Eaton came into the picture. She had been a barmaid but later married a man who Jackson appointed to his cabinet. Naturally he felt very kindly to Mrs. Eaton and he talked Martin Van Buren into being nice to her. With that the gauntlet was laid down. Jackson made it plain that if Mrs. Calhoun did not accept Mrs. Eaton into society, Calhoun was going to get the axe. The story goes that he discussed it with Mrs. Calhoun and she said, "I'll give you my decision tomorrow morning."

They got up in the morning and she said, "I'll not accept her under any conditions." He said, "I agree with you and I will never be president of the United States." So Martin Van Buren became president of the United States.

Another thing I don't think most people know is that Calhoun and Jackson were mortal enemies. They despised each other. Although they were both Southerners, their thoughts and beliefs were entirely different. One was a nationalist and the other a states' righter. Under the Constitution of the United States anyone has the right to secede from the Union. Anybody who knows anything about the United States Constitution knows that—except the United States Supreme Court.

During Jackson's presidency they had a banquet. Jackson was seated at the head of the table and Calhoun at the other end. Jackson raised his glass and said, "The Union, it must be preserved."

Calhoun stood up, raised his wine glass and said, "The Union, next to our liberty, most dear."

I wish I knew as much about Kirby-Smith as I do about Calhoun. I know more about his record as a Confederate general in the Civil War than I do anything else. It is a well-known fact that at the first battle of Manassas [Bull Run] he saved the *day. Had Jefferson Davis listened to his generals [they] could have marched into Washington and taken that city.*

Everyone thought that slavery was the issue during the Civil War. Nothing could be further from the truth. The vast majority of slaves were owned by wealthy people. The average Southerner didn't have any money to buy a slave. They were poor working people.

The issue in the war was over states' rights, which Calhoun supported. He was the one who wrote the bill of nullification. What the Northern states tried to do was impose tariff laws upon them, which hurt the South, an agrarian society, and helped the North, an industrial society. The rich Southern planters were the ones who owned the slaves. Everybody thinks that every Southerner who owned a slave was a Simon Legree. Well, nothing could be further from the truth. They fed them, they clothed them, they did everything for them. They kept the families together. This is historic fact.

Calhoun owned slaves himself. At one time he owned one thousand slaves. I've been up to the quarters there, and I've seen places down in Central America that you wouldn't believe. The slaves lived like kings compared to those places in Honduras, Nicaragua and El Salvador. Slavery was wrong; there is no question about it. In Calhoun's judgment slavery would have been abolished eventually. A lot of people thought that had he lived, the war would never have been fought.

In 1979 my sister and I presented a painting of my great-great-grandfather to the governor of South Carolina. There was my wife and myself, one of my daughters, my sister and one of her children. We were invited to visit the Senate while it was in session.

Without me knowing anything about it, they introduced the Calhoun family from Florida. The governor asked me to come up and make a statement. Well, if you had hit me with a wet mop in the face I couldn't have been more surprised. I got up and I thanked them very cordially and said that even though all of us present were native Floridians, we do deeply appreciate our ancestry from the state of South Carolina. When I said that, the whole Senate chamber stood up and applauded.

John C. Calhoun (1782–1850) was elected vice-president in 1824 with John Quincy Adams as president. In 1828 he was reelected with Andrew Jackson as president. In an age when the vice-presidency went to the man with the second highest number of votes, Calhoun was the only person to be elected under two different presidents.

Benjamin Alexander Putnam (1801–1869) was a lawyer, a judge, a soldier and a member of the Florida legislature. He arrived in St. Augustine in 1821, at the time of transfer from Spanish to United States' rule. He became affiliated with Judge Joseph Lee Smith, the first federally appointed judge in the new territory. Smith and his wife Frances Kirby-Smith were the parents of Confederate general Edmund Kirby-Smith, who was born in the Aviles Street house in 1824.

Two of Frances's sisters, Catherine Anne and Helen, also found their way to Florida. The youngest, Helen, married Benjamin A. Putnam. Their daughter Kate Kirby Putnam married John C. Calhoun Jr., thus uniting three families.

Kate and John's son was Noble Putnam Calhoun's grandfather, Benjamin Alexander Putnam Calhoun, who married Julia Catherine Peterman. Their son, Edward Noble Calhoun, married the daughter of Gertrude de Medici and William A. MacWilliams, thus adding the Minorcan lineage.

An article in the March 22–28, 1990 issue of *Compass* magazine discusses the Kirby-Smith family in more detail, noting that Helen and Frances, as well as Catherine's daughter, were loyal to the Confederacy and frequently passed on information gleaned from Union soldiers.

May 31, 1990

The Lyon building on King and St. George Streets was empty and abandoned for years until recently restored as upscale condominiums. The St. Augustine Historical Society research library now functions from the former Kirby-Smith home. It is called Seguie/Kirby Smith House, in recognition of the Minorcan family residing there prior to the Smith family.

BLACK HISTORY IN FOCUS
Elmo Slappy

E lmo Slappy is a St. Augustine native who returned to his hometown after living thirty years in New York. He experienced the 1920s in St. Augustine, a time when the first known black photographer in the city, Richard Aloysius Twine (1896–1974), was recording the people and places of Lincolnville on glass negatives.

The collection of glass plates was discovered in 1988 in a house that was about to be demolished. Fortunately, the valuable find was turned over to the St. Augustine Historical Society and prints were made by Kenneth Barrett Jr.

Armed with the prints, anthropologists Dr. Patricia Griffin and Diana Edwards searched for identifications. Elmo Slappy saw the faces of his past in the pictures. As he looked at the above photo of an elaborately decorated parlor, Slappy pointed to the portrait on the wall. "This is Will Martin," he explained. "He was the first Negro to own his own bar here." He pointed to the woman in the background. "That must be his wife."

Although Mr. Slappy knew Richard Twine, he said Twine never took his picture. The following is his story told prior to leafing through the photographs a second time.

I was born right here in St. Augustine in 1902 (I'm eighty-six). I was born on Moore Street and I went to Excelsior High School. Professor Chairs was the principal at

Excelsior. It was a lovely school. My sisters and brothers all went there too. We were all members of St. Paul's AME Church, which I joined in 1913. F.D. Richardson was the pastor there.

Everybody was very close here. We were afraid to talk about anyone in case it was a relative. As a young man I had a taxi service I started in 1923. It was a sightseeing service. I drove a big seven-passenger Hudson car and charged three dollars an hour. I did that until 1928.

My father used to drive a horse and carriage around sightseeing. He did that for a lifetime. This town and Palatka were the only two towns where Negroes could ride with white people. I always took around the people from the Ponce de Leon Hotel and the Alcazar [hotel]. I drove the white people to Jacksonville, too, when they wanted to go. I would take them all over—to the beach or the Alligator Farm—wherever they wanted.

One of the people I remember from that time is Uncle Bucky. He was a fine person, a good citizen. He had a barn behind his house on Central Avenue where he used to give barn dances for everyone.

My mother's name was Elizabeth Slappy and my father was John Slappy. He came here from Americus, Georgia. My mother was born here in St. Augustine on Washington Street. Her maiden name was Jones. There were seven of us: three boys and four girls. The boys were James, Herbert and me [Elmo]. The girls were Annie, Claudia, Johnny and Alice. I was the fifth born.

I moved to New York and lived there until 1950. I had a limousine that I drove for the United Nations for the Pakistani government. I drove them around for eleven years. The man I drove around was called [phonetically spelled] *Sassa Foola Khan, but don't ask me to spell it for you. I enjoyed doing that. Later I had a barbershop. I had that for fifteen years. Then I came back here. I lived with my sister Johnny Young on Kings Ferry Way.*

When I came I re-opened the Iceberg. That was the store owned by Arthur Forward back in the '20s. It was a combination drug store and ice cream parlor on Bridge Street. Mr. Forward made all kinds of ice cream. He could make just about anything you wanted. The Record *company [St. Augustine Record] was his main customer. He supplied all the employees of the* Record *with ice cream. My store was also a combination drug store and ice cream parlor, but I didn't make my own ice cream.*

Later I moved to a place on Central Avenue and De Haven. It was a confectionary store. I called it the Big Dipper and I sold ice cream and all that to the children. The children kept me open. This wasn't a bad place to grow up in. I had a good childhood.

Slappy identified the twins as Tee and Helen Saxon. "They were younger than me," he said. "You couldn't tell them apart when they were little, but after they grew up you could."

A 1924 city directory shows the Iceberg on 74 Bridge Street (the southwest corner of Bridge and Washington Streets), Snyders at 55 Bridge (the *Record* parking lot) and Frank Butler's Palace Market at 87 Washington, south of the intersection.

"Slappy," as he is called at the Council on Aging, drives his 1965 Cadillac to lunch every day, and sings and plays drums in the council's rhythm band.

February 7, 1991

Additional information about photographs printed from the glass negatives can be obtained through the St. Augustine Historical Society.

A CONNECTICUT YANKEE MEETS A MINORCAN

Norma Perry Martin

N orma Martin is a St. Augustine native of Minorcan and Yankee descent. In 1817 she married Otis Martin, a farmer from Elkton, and shared farm life with him until 1925 when the family returned to St. Augustine and she began to work at Florida East Coast Railroad (FEC). She was an employee of FEC for thirty-seven years and a member of Memorial Presbyterian Church for seventy-three. This is one of Mrs. Martin's favorite stories relating to the Civil War romance of her Minorcan ancestor, Margarita Antonia Capo, seen above, and Margarita's Yankee-soldier husband, Roscoe Perry.

The story begins with the Civil War when my grandfather was a Yankee soldier who belonged to the 17th Connecticut Regulars and was captured at the battle of Gettysburg. He was put in a horrible prison in Richmond where he stayed for eighteen months before he was exchanged for a Southern prisoner and rejoined his regiment. Then he was sent to Jacksonville, Florida, with the idea of coming down to St. Augustine to capture the city. Now, the officials of St. Augustine knew that the Yankees were coming down the waterway, so they met them at the seawall right across the street about where Churchill's Restaurant is now. St. Augustine surrendered over a flag of truce and my grandfather, being the commanding officer, stepped out on the seawall and accepted the flag of truce—

accepted it with a salute—and marched down the bay front to the barracks at Marine Street. Some of the soldiers were stationed at the barracks; some of them were stationed at the fort because there was not enough room for them at the barracks.

That was in 1863. They stayed here for the duration of the war. Now, one of the things the soldiers had to do was march with a little fife and drum corps up and down the bay front. They would start from about Cordova Street and go all the way down to the end, turn around and march back up the other side of the street. My grandmother, who was a Capo, [her name was Margarita Capo—she was of Minorcan descent] *used to watch the soldiers march. Her people lived in a little clapboard house, right there where Churchill's* [restaurant] *is now. It had a little white picket fence. So, my grandfather, marching with his saber, fell in love with my grandmother over that white picket fence. She was a beautiful Minorcan girl and I was told that once she winked at him. The rest happened something like this.*

One day my grandmother was out cleaning the front yard. They never did plant flowers in the front yard; instead they kept it swept fresh and clean. They made their own brooms and my grandmother was out cleaning the front yard with this homemade broom when this soldier came up to the yard with a bundle of laundry under his arm. He asked my grandmother if she knew someone who could do some laundry for him. So she said, "I have to go in and ask my mother." They did all their own washing, you know, and with the war they could use some extra money so Margarita's mother said, "You go ahead and do the laundry for him." Of course, there was the war and all the able-bodied men were sent to battle and the family had to make a dollar any way they could.

Well, my great-grandfather, my mother's father, did not go into the war because he was a cripple. So he stayed home. My grandfather, Roscoe Charles Perry, asked my grandfather Capo if he could come and give attention to my grandmother. And my grandfather said, "Yes." When the war ended in 1865 my grandmother and grandfather were engaged, but he had to go back to Connecticut to be mustered out. He came back then in 1866 and they were married that year by a civilian justice of the peace. She was Catholic and he was Protestant, so they couldn't have a ceremony in the cathedral. It was then they bought the house at 52 St. George Street, which is now the Museum of Yesterday's Toys. That house was originally built back in the 1760s and was a one-story coquina house. Then during the British occupation from 1763 to 1783 they built a second floor. After my grandfather bought the house he started a little grocery store on the bottom floor and my father was their first child, born in one of the upstairs rooms of that house. That was in...let me see...1867.

You know St. George Street was nothing but a dirt road and when my grandfather had to go to Jacksonville to buy produce for his store it was an all-day trip with a

The Roscoe Perry family surrounded by orange trees on their Noda Concession property. *From left*: Margaret, Charles, Helen, Mary S. William, Margarita (Mrs. Perry) and Roscoe Perry. *Courtesy of Eleanor Philips Barnes*

horse and a wagon. So while he was gone to Jacksonville my grandmother had to take care of the store. In the corner of the store there was a big syrup keg and one day when my grandfather was away and my father was about two years old—you know what two-year-olds are like, always getting into things—well, he turned on the spigot on that thing and when my grandmother found it the syrup was all over the floor. Well, she dared not let my grandfather come home and see that thing because he was a red-haired Connecticut Yankee and had the temper to go with it. So she took a clean cloth, sopped up what she could and squeezed it back in the barrel. She got up all the nitty-gritty and washed up the floor and my grandfather never knew about it.

Sometime later my grandfather got the idea he wanted to plant some orange trees. So he bought three lots right behind where the Ripley's museum is now. He bought them from Dr. Peck. He filled those lots with orange trees and he built a two-story house there. But then in 1885 a freeze killed the trees and bankrupted him. I don't know how long they lived there but I think it was until my father became a young man. There's a picture of the family sitting along the orange grove over there when my father was a boy, so they must have been there some years.

My grandfather lived to a ripe old age and fathered quite a family—three girls and two boys. Later the family lived at 33 Water Street where I was born.

Margarita Antonia Capo (1847–1923) was a descendant of Juan Capo, a native of Minorca and one of the several hundred emigrants from the ill-fated Turnbull colony in New Smyrna. Mrs. Eleanor Philips Barnes, a first cousin of Mrs. Martin, was also born at 33 Water Street. Mrs. Barnes remembers additional details about the courtship of Margarita Capo. According to Mrs. Barnes, Roscoe Perry was required to sit in a chair at least two feet away from his intended. As the two lovers conversed, the family circled the room keeping a watchful eye on the young couple.

The house at 52 St. George Street, known as the Rodriguez-Avero-Sanchez House, is on the National Register of Historic Places. The original one-room structure dates back to about 1753. Over the years various additions and modifications were completed until the building reached the stage of development the newly married Perrys enjoyed. The first-floor rooms were frequently used as stores after Roscoe Perry left the grocery business.

Records show that in March 1862, a Union flagship anchored off the St. Augustine inlet. Mayor Cristobal Bravo prudently raised a white flag over Fort Marion (Castillo de San Marcos) and soon a small boat sailed to the seawall with the passenger, Commander C.R.P. Rodgers, carrying a flag of truce. The flag of truce was accepted by Mayor Bravo, with a group of council members and Unionists looking on. They, and perhaps other passengers in the boat, marched to the fort to raise the Stars and Stripes.

Although the original occupation was by a unit from New Hampshire, later troops from the Connecticut Volunteers arrived including sixteen musicians (probably a fife and drum corps).

It is also worth noting that during the occupation, soldiers were quartered at St. Francis Barracks with the overflow residing in tents on the terreplein of the fort.

February 4, 1988

Churchill's Attic is now Harry's Restaurant and still a popular eating establishment on the bay front. The building at 52 St. George Street is a restored historic building called the Rodriguez-Avero-Sanchez House and functions as Casa Rodriguez, a jewelry store and specialty shop.

Photo by Karen Harvey

CIVIL RIGHTS MOVEMENT 1964
Henry and Katherine "Kat" Twine

Henry Twine, retired postal employee who, at the time of this interview, was currently serving his sixth year as county commissioner, and his wife of forty-one years, Katherine (seen above), both were active participants in the civil rights movement of the 1960s. Now, twenty-four years after the notorious "summer of '64" both Henry and "Kat" look back at those difficult days not with bitterness but, instead, with a conviction that it is time to see the humorous side to some of the activities. Here are their stories.

HENRY

We actually started in 1963 when Dr. Robert Hayling of the NAACP, who was advisor to the youth involved in the movement, came down to stage sit-ins. The first sit-in was by a young black fellow named Henry Thomas who tried to get served at the Woolworth counter. They didn't know what to do with him so they turned the lights out at the lunch counter and called the sheriff. They arrested him and put him in jail. Later they let him out but they said he was crazy and wanted to send him to Chattahoochee, but he screamed and yelled and raised so much cain they decided not to do that, so they put him back in jail.

We operated under the NAACP, who sent representatives down. We practiced non-violent demonstrations and went out on night marches. After a while it cooled off for that summer and very little activity went on in the wintertime. The first part of March, Martin Luther King [Jr.] was in Orlando and we went down to see him. We never did get to see him but we talked to C.T. Vivian, Andy Young and Hosea Williams, his lieutenants, and they persuaded him to come to town. About that time we switched from NAACP to SCLC [Southern Christian Leadership Conference] *and after a while all hell broke loose.*

KAT

The first time I went to jail was during the Easter holidays. I was the first adult female to be arrested. They arrested me at the Monson hotel. I was with a fellow from Florida Memorial College, Jimmy Jackson, and two white fellows from the University of Florida. We stayed in jail that night and in the morning we had to go before Judge Mathis. They bailed us out right away that time.

I always kept my suitcase packed so I would be ready. They would come out at night to pick you up. They wouldn't pick you up during the day. On Mother's Day I decided to hide out so I could be with my mother that day. I turned myself in the next morning and they put me back in jail. I was in jail about four times. One of those times Mrs. [Malcolm] *Peabody came in. She was the mother of the governor of Massachusetts. She sat-in with one of her white friends and another lady that looked like she was white. They were all served and Mrs. Peabody asked, "Do you serve black folks in here?" And they said, "No, we don't." So she said, "My friend here is black." So they arrested them and I was there when they arrived. They stayed in until they were bonded out. The children gave the ladies their bunks to lie down on. I always had a bunk by myself because the children said I snored so they wouldn't sleep with me.*

The mother of one of the white boys with me came down and I told him, "You're really going to catch it now." But she went to Judge Mathis and told him she raised her boy right and she was proud of him. She raised so much cain hitting on his desk they had to take her out.

We all were found guilty and had to appear before Judge Bryant Simpson in federal court. He was very nice. One of the lawyers asked, "When are you going to give that Twine woman some time [off]*?" because I had been in jail so much. I never did have to stay in three or four days at a time. I never did eat the prison food. They used to slide a metal tray under the door, but I wouldn't eat it. A prison trustee used to bring it to me.*

HENRY

We were pretty well organized once we got started. Martin Luther King would come in once a week or once every two or three weeks. Andy Young and Hosea Williams ran the operations. Every night we would plan something different to do the next day.

Henry Twine smiles in his campaign photo when he ran for city commissioner and then mayor. *Courtesy of the Willie Galimore Center*

We attracted quite a few local white people and we wrote to colleges to ask students to come down and spend the Easter break with us and go to jail. You'd be surprised at the response we had. We must have had over five hundred to a thousand here. Some of the merchants were very nice to us. They would donate food. We had a kitchen set up over at the Elks Club and we got some army cots for them to sleep.

We always tried to plan something different and one day during the summer we had an idea about the Monson. There was a group of Jewish Rabbis here from New York. They checked in at the Monson and the plan was to get some black females to go swimming with them over at the Monson Motor Lodge. So we sent up to Savannah to get some young black ladies—Hosea Williams was originally from Atlanta and he knew most every body from up there.

King and Williams and Andy Young were standing on the seawall watching while the Rabbis were creating a fuss. Nobody was paying any attention to King; they were all watching the Rabbis. After awhile they called the police because of all the excitement and, of course, they came right away. But then a car pulled up and the black ladies jumped out and jumped into the swimming pool. They all had their bathing suits on and the Rabbis had their suits on under their clothes and they jumped in. Then one of the local policemen jumped in with all his clothes on, even his pistol. But he couldn't get them out. Finally the Monson manager ran in and got a barrel of [muriatic] acid and poured it into the pool. It didn't do any good though and it didn't hurt anybody.

So that night we all sat around and planned what to do next. We weren't going to go back to that pool. But the next morning we went by there and, guess what!

There was this big old alligator swimming around in the Monson pool. We didn't care, though. We had something else planned for that day anyway.

Yes, those were tough times, but, you know, there really were some funny moments. We can't forget. Like the Holocaust, we should never forget. But we can remember with humor.

The incident described by Henry Twine, as well as other factual accounts of the civil rights movement of the 1960s can be found in a comprehensive account of St. Augustine's black history in *Racial Change and Community Crisis: St. Augustine, Florida 1877–1980* by David R. Colburn, Columbia University Press, 1985.

February 25, 1988

Henry Twine served on the city commission from 1983 to 1992. Before his death in 1994, the street on which he lived was renamed Twine Street. In January 2002, Katherine "Kat" Twine was present for the presentation of a marker for the Great Floridian 2000, in honor of her husband. She died in December of that year.

SPANISH LEGEND
Eleanor Philips Barnes

Eleanor Philips Barnes is without doubt the most prolific genealogical researcher in our ancient city. During her decades of searching through birth and marriage records, deeds, musty files and crumbling papers she has documented family trees for descendants of St. Augustine residents who lived through many historical events in the city. While producing records for family interest, Mrs. Barnes uncovered facts that enriched our understanding of the heritage of the city. The spices that enhanced the flavor of these facts are the legends passed down through the generations adding mystery, intrigue and romance to the ancestral history. Some legends are well known to old families here, others are not. All are worth repeating.

In this romantic tale, Brigita Arrendondo, one-time mistress of the Horruytiner House, claims to be able to communicate with the spirits of former mistresses. The loggia of the house is seen in the photo above.

The Lindsey House at 214 St. George Street, also known as the Don Pedro Horruytiner House, had many mistresses. The first mistress that I know of was Mrs. Horruytiner. She was Don Pedro's wife—we use the term "mistress" in an old fashioned sense. Her name was Maria Ruiz. The second mistress was their son's wife, Antonia. She was from a very noted family in St. Augustine. The third woman was Mrs. Fernando de La Meza Arrendondo. Mrs. Arrendondo

was Brigita Gomez and had been married to Mateo Guaterama and had several children with him. Fernando Arrendondo—he was a handsome man—was first married to Dona Antonia, Brigita's aunt. When Dona Antonia died, Fernando married Brigita, who was a widow by that time. It was quite a love match. Brigita loved that house and particularly loved that garden.

Now, this story takes place in 1821, when the American government took over Florida and Florida became a territory of the United States. Fernando was not happy with the American incursion. He didn't like it here at all. In fact, he didn't agree with the changes and he didn't get along with any of the Americans. He wanted to go back to Cuba where he could feel more at home in familiar surroundings. But Brigita didn't want to go. She didn't want to go at all. She begged him to let her have the house, to give it to her and not sell it.

Fernando finally promised he would not sell the house right away. Instead, he would give it to her if she would give up this nonsensical notion that she could see and talk with the former mistresses of the house, Mrs. Horruytiner and Antonia, which she said she could do. So, as the story goes, Brigita stopped mentioning her communications with the mistresses, but she probably continued to think about them. Probably while she tended the beautiful yellow roses that grew so profusely in her garden.

One day she was seated in her lovely garden, amidst all those gorgeous roses dreaming and wishing about going back in history to meet the ladies that had lived there. Perhaps she fell asleep and dreamed this, but it is said Maria Ruiz appeared to her and talked of her beautiful roses and how she, too, had planted lovely flowers. So Brigita picked the roses and gave her a bouquet of them and they talked awhile. Finally, Maria asked if Brigita wanted to meet her daughter-in-law and she called Antonia out to meet her. And, oh, she was so thrilled. They all talked for a while and then the first two mistresses of the house left.

Fernando came home anticipating that Brigita would have been preparing for guests they were expecting for dinner. He couldn't understand why she wasn't dressed and when she tried to explain he refused to believe her. He went off to get her a glass of wine and while he was doing that a good friend, Mr. Alverez, dropped by. Brigita told Mr. Alverez about her experience and he, too, refused to believe her.

"My dear lady," he said, "It is just a figment of your imagination. Try to put it away from you."

She said, "He has promised me the house. I want the house. I don't want to give it up. But, this was so real."

They talked for a while and finally he left her. As he reached the gate he stepped on a bouquet of roses—freshly picked yellow roses. Slowly he returned to the house. "You must have dropped these," he suggested softly presenting the bouquet to Brigita.

Her face was pale as she held the flowers tenderly, whispering only, "Maria's roses. Maria's yellow roses."

The ownership of the Horruytiner House has been thoroughly documented. Don Pedro Alcantara Benedict Horruytiner y Puevo did indeed live in the house in 1763, selling it the following year to a Spaniard, Juan Elixio de la Puente, who had been appointed by the king to dispose of Spanish property at the outset of the British Period. The house changed hands many times until it was purchased by Fernando de La Maza Arrendondo in 1801. Arrendondo was an aide to Governor Vincente Manuel de Zespedes and probably did keep his promise to Brigita. The house was not sold until 1839, when Virginia Watson purchased the structure by auction.

The individuals named in this legend also have been thoroughly documented. The basis for the apparition, however, I leave for the reader to determine.

February 16, 1988

Although ownership of the historic home has changed over the years, it remains one of the city's significant colonial structures.

Photo by Karen Harvey

TEENAGE YEARS IN THE 1930S
Edward Brubaker

The Reverend Mr. Edward Brubaker, DD, spent his high school years and college vacation days in St. Augustine while his father, the Reverend Mr. L.E. Brubaker, served as minister of Memorial Presbyterian Church from 1931 to 1943. For much of that time the family lived in the manse at 32 Sevilla Street.

In 1941 Brubaker was ordained at Memorial Presbyterian with his father and ordained brother officiating. In September 1991 he returned to the church on the occasion of the fiftieth anniversary celebration of his ordination. He is seen in the above photo with his wife in front of Memorial Presbyterian Church.

During those fifty years he was pastor of various churches, served a term as navy chaplain, was director of the Westminster Foundation in the Philadelphia area and was Synod executive for the Synod of Mid-America. After retirement in 1985, he was a volunteer on a mission in Trinidad.

The following are his recollections of his years in St. Augustine.

We moved here in 1931. The original idea was to replace Dr. Bigler, the minister who was very beloved, but had not been well. They called my father to come as the associate pastor with the clear plan that within a year or two Dr. Bigler would retire and my father would become the senior minister.

In fact, my father had resigned the church in Birmingham, Alabama, because of this and had accepted the call. Then the church here changed its mind slightly, because Dr. Bigler was better, and then because of the crash, I guess, and lack of funds, they asked my father to wait. So, instead of coming in 1929 as originally planned, we came in 1931.

Of course, the Biglers were living here in the manse and we rented a house, which, to my delight as a landlubber from Birmingham, Alabama, was on the water. It was three blocks north of the fort—I think on Mulberry, but I'm not sure of the name.

Right on the end of the street there was water. In fact, when we had northeasters sometimes we had to figure out when we could get out of the house because the water would come up in the yard at high tide. But we knew it would go out at low tide. So we would go out and get the groceries or whatever we needed then. And it had lots of palm trees. Because I had never lived with the water or in a subtropical climate, I loved it there.

I was thirteen years old [when we arrived] *and had a crisis immediately. We moved here in January. In Birmingham they started a new class in September and a new class in January. When we came here in January, I was finishing my freshman year in high school, which meant I either had to go back a half year or suddenly jump ahead a half year.*

The principal said, "Well, why not try going ahead a half year. Here are the books for the sophomore year. You have three weeks to see what you can do with them."

I did manage to pass all the exams except Latin. Miss Cavin was the Latin teacher at that time. I had to do Latin in summer school to catch up with that. So I was a sophomore when we came in '31. There was a teacher I had who was greatly loved, but I can't remember her name. She was a physics teacher. She had kind of blonde hair and was lots of fun and a very good teacher. I remember that class, and I remember the principal Mr. Crookshank, who taught chemistry. That was one of my least favorite subjects.

The trouble was Sally Burt Nuzum, whom I was dating at that time. Billy McGuire and I shared one of the chemistry tables together. And we enjoyed each other's company too much. The work wasn't that hard, but I was color blind and when we had all these tests of identification by color I said, "I'll do the work and y'all tell me what color it is." There was no way I could tell. Mr. Crookshank did not appreciate that. We really did talk too much. I got a B plus instead of an A. But we enjoyed the classes. It was a small high school.

One of the things that happened to me here had to do with the violin. I had been playing violin in Birmingham for seven years in public school, which had a very advanced system of school music. I came here and there was not a string teacher in the

The house that had been home to the Brubaker children is now used for church offices and meeting rooms. *Photo by Karen Harvey*

city. But in those days, you know, no matter how much money was left, the Ponce de Leon Hotel was kept open a certain number of months a year.

That year they brought down a string quintet from New York that played the dinner music in the big dining room and for the dances. On Sunday evenings they gave a classical or semi-classical concert and people from the town were allowed to come and sit in the outer circle of the main lobby.

Well, I loved music greatly. I had studied violin. I did a violin minor in college for the fun of it. I gradually got acquainted with Mr. Gunter, who was the first violin and the leader of the group. I visited with him as a young high school kid. He was very nice and he was very kind to me. Finally, after a year or so, I asked my parents if I could ask him to teach me since there was no string teacher in St. Augustine. We had heard about the New York teachers who charged twenty-five dollars a lesson. Think about twenty-five dollars in the '30s. Remember this was the bottom of the Depression.

My parents said, "Well, you can ask him, but you have got to find out what it will cost." So I asked him and he said he would teach me, but he wouldn't tell me what it would cost. "Well," they said, "you can go to the first class but you have got to find out what it will cost."

He never charged me anything. And he never taught anyone else in town. He was merciless in a certain way, but was a very good teacher. You know what he did the first several weeks? I had already played several years, but he made me play nothing but open strings. I had to get to where I could take sixty seconds for one down-bow and one up-bow and not jerk. But you see, that was the basis of a legato tone. And then afterward he was watching everything—my arms held right, my wrists—but I enjoyed studying with him.

The family lived two or three years on the waterfront before we moved into the manse. We acquired a sailboat we tied up in the front yard. We would haul it up at full moon to scrape the barnacles off and paint it. Then we put it in at the next high tide. My brother Lauren and I greatly enjoyed the sailboat. I cannot remember the Methodist minister's name, but a couple of local shipbuilders had built a sailboat for themselves. They got tired of it and one of them sold his half of the boat to the Methodist minister's son for thirty dollars. Then later on, the other fellow got tired of it and sold it to us for the same amount.

The Methodist minister's son and we owned it and tied it up where we lived. Then the Methodist minister's son went off to college and sold us his part for $5. So we got the whole boat for $35. We sailed it for ten years and sold it for $150.

One time we took a class friend out, Rubye Lee Moeller. My brother and I had dated her some. Rubye Lee's parents were dead set against her going sailing because she couldn't swim. We said, "come on, let's go sailing!"

This boat, you could keel it way over and let the water come in and it wouldn't turn over. On this occasion we keeled over a little too far and it turned over. I was doing some life saving on her while my brother bailed it out and turned it over. Well, her parents weren't supposed to know she had been sailing, so we docked the boat and went to the house and my mother helped us while we dried out all of Rubye Lee's clothes and ironed them so her parents wouldn't know. [In Rubye Lee's version of the story, Brubaker, an expert swimmer swam her to a nearby yacht where she waited safely while they righted the sailboat. She said she never was afraid and often laughs about the incident.]

The boat didn't have a name when we first got it. We decided the name needed to be euphonious; it should not be immediately transparent as to its meaning, and it should be fitting for a sailboat. We finally named it Pranayama. What that means is breath control, or wind control. It was euphonious, fitting for a sailboat and certainly not immediately apparent as to its meaning. In addition to that we put the name on the boat in Sanskrit. If you think about it, Sanskrit looks enough like our kind of printing so you look at it and think something is wrong with your eyes. You look at it and think, "Why can't I read this?" We loved it.

When the tide was more than half full the bridge had to open for us to go through. The bridge tender was supposed to record the names of all the boats that went through, and he had a terrible time with us. He would squint at this thing as we disappeared in the distance. He would shout, "What is the 'blankity-blank' name of that boat?"

Also, that was the days of Prohibition. We called the boat the "Bru" as a nickname, because that was what people called my father. But they put it in the paper that the minister's sons and their boat, the "Brew," won third place.

We also had a funny thing at the manse when Prohibition was over. The manse phone number and the number of some bar that also sold liquor was almost the same. Once in a while people would call up and immediately start giving us this long order for whiskey and everything. And then they'd give their name and they were members of the church. Then we would say, "Well, thank you, but this is the Presbyterian manse."

It wasn't until after Dr. Bigler did resign that we did move into the manse. Again, remember it was the bottom of the Depression and the Biglers had been here many years. If you can imagine this lovely house—all the walls were gray. They had not been painted for twenty years. The church was very poor at that point. Only the upkeep of the church was endowed and that was endowed in Florida East Coast Railway bonds, so that was in the hands of receivers at that point. There was almost no income. They couldn't redecorate the manse and my father, who liked to do this sort of thing, volunteered. He said if they would buy the paint he and his sons (my brother and me) would paint it. We spent a summer changing it from gray to a light color. I'm color blind, but I guess it was close to what you have now.

It took three coats to do it. My brother and father cheerfully assigned me the job of doing all the filigree work and the fireplaces and the baseboards and trim around the window. We had a good time doing it. The only time I had a painter's problem was when I was painting a closet in the middle bedroom. There was a lot of space above the door where the fumes were caught. The first thing I knew I could barely get off the ladder and I lay down on the floor and I felt like I was still trembling. It took awhile for me to overcome it.

We didn't have a refrigerator then. We only had an old icebox. We didn't even have a stove. We had a fireless cooker. It was like a hole lined with aluminum and a top that fits down tightly. And you have soap stones where you heat. It was the same idea as a crockpot. It went back to the turn of the century, but my mother still had it. She figured out that if we could cook in it we could make ice cream in it. And that became my Sunday morning job. Before breakfast I sat on the back steps there and crushed the ice in a gunnysack. Then you have the ice cream in a three-pound coffee can, and you just take the vessel that you normally put the meat in, and that left an area all the way around for the salt and ice. And, of course, just sitting there it would tend to become icy. Then between Sunday school and church I'd come over and pour off the excess, open up the top and stir it up a little bit and put a little more ice in it. By noon we had a three-pound coffee can full of ice cream. It was enough for then, and we could keep some for that night.

Lorenzo Pratt Oviatt was the full-time church choir director and organist while we were here. He goes back before my time. I think he was a graduate of Yale. He really knew his music. During the season he gave evening concerts once a month or every two weeks and everybody would come to the organ recitals. You know those Grecian lamps at the end of the pews? They used to have gas in them. And it was just for the vesper services that the two gas jets were lit. The organ, which had been a Roosevelt organ, was rebuilt as an Estey organ. Every so often Mr. Oviatt would say, "Ed, it's about time to give them the treatment." What that meant was, it made him furious that people talked during the prelude. His "treatment" consisted of playing very, very soft, and then getting louder and louder. And the louder and louder he would get the louder they would get. Then suddenly he would take a measure's rest and they were all left shouting in the silence.

Let me tell you my organ story. [Although not an experienced organist, young Brubaker occasionally filled in during the off-season when Oviatt was away.] *When the Estey organ was rebuilt from the old Roosevelt they really put in a console that was designed for a theater organ. There was a panel across the top with these little buttons across it. And if you punched it a light would come on and that indicated the stop was on. It was like the theater in the dark.*

There are five divisions. The swell, the great and the choir were behind the big organ façade. Then in the north of the hall were all the reeds, trumpets, fagottos, clarions and all like that. Down in the south end, under the lovely rose window, was the echo organ. It had the chimes and some very soft strings. My father liked to have what he called rustle music. You know, when you finish the hymn before the sermon people make a lot of noise sitting down and slamming the books in the racks. So when you complete the hymn you change to some soft cover music while the people sit down.

Well, the hymn before the sermon had been a very heroic one and I loved gradually building it up and finally I had the tubas and clarion and swell, the great and the choir—I had the whole thing going. It was a very victorious hymn. You see there were five divisions, but there are only four keyboards. The solo organ and the echo organ played off the same board. But you could preset what you wanted. A button could be pushed that said solo organ off, echo organ on, and it would immediately preset what you set for the echo organ.

Now, I had chosen a nice phrase from a Bach B minor symphony that I was going to play on the echo organ—a little rustle music after the hymn. I had it all preset, but the one thing I didn't know was that here in Florida, unfortunately, the electrical connections were all underground and sometimes they worked and sometimes they didn't. So I punched solo organ off, echo organ on. I put my hands down and I expected this barely audible sound and WHAMMMM! It came out with all the strength of the former hymn.

All the people used to sit in that end up there under the tubas and all the reeds. I hit this full when they were halfway down and they stood right back up. I jerked my hands off immediately and almost fell off the bench. By the time I figured out what had happened there was no graceful way to back up. I just turned it off and hoped for better luck next time. I really shouldn't have been playing anyway.

About the house, I remember all the fireplaces were functioning. We only used the third floor for storage. It had previously been used for servants' quarters. The bedroom at the back, over the formal living room was the master bedroom. My grandmother, who lived with us, had the big middle room. And then in the back was the bedroom we used. We were as far away from our parents as possible. It was very convenient. Though we loved them very much, we were college age at the time, and if we came in very late, we could come up the back steps and not disturb them.

It was a fine old house. We enjoyed it. Mother enjoyed entertaining here. She always had the women in. They had what was called a praise service here. They had chairs set up and then she would serve fancy refreshments. I remember she had some kind of cranberry ice.

This was the dining room [now a conference room and Pastor Ed Albright's office] *and this was a kind of a sitting room* [now church office]. *Then beyond that where Dr. Hunter's study is, it was the library. While my father had a study in the church house, he had a lot of his books and a desk right in there. You know, in the early days they never even took up an offering in the church. They had plates at the door you could put something in, but the rest Flagler just paid for. Which was a terrible thing. It was while my father was here that ceased to be. It was the best thing that ever happened to the church.*

Flagler no longer supported the church. It was the first time the people began to support it. They could have supported it, but they never had been trained to do it. They hadn't really seriously thought about stewardship and weren't pledging $200 a month or $3,000 a year. They just put a few dollars in the plate. My memory is that there was a congregation of about four hundred at the time.

I think the church and my family all influenced me to become a minister. I think that in those formative years this church did influence my decisions.

A *Record* article on August 17, 1941, noted that the ordination of Charles Edward Brubaker would follow the 8:00 p.m. Union Service. The article stated the Reverend Lauren E. Brubaker Jr. would preach the service conducted by the two brothers' father. It went on to say, "The occasion is unique in the annals of Memorial Presbyterian Church, and probably in most other churches with a father and two sons participating." It was also noted that the music was provided by Lorenzo P. Oviatt.

The 32 Sevilla Street house was built by oil millionaire Henry Flagler for his chief lieutenant James E. Ingraham (1830–1924). In addition to serving as vice-president of the Florida East Coast Railway, and president of the Model Land Company, Ingraham held a number of civic and political positions including mayor of the city. Constructed in 1894 in Colonial Revival style, the two-and-a-half-story building is considered the finest surviving example in the city of that architectural style.

In 1925, after Ingraham's death, the house was sold to Flagler heiress Louise Wise Lewis. It was her desire that the house always remain the manse (the pastor's home) for Memorial Presbyterian Church. Prior to that time the building beside the church had served as the manse.

Around 1989 it was determined that the building could satisfy the need for more space required by the growing congregation. The Lewis heirs agreed to change the usage, as long as the building always carried the name "manse." In March 1990, before the church celebrated its centennial, the building was dedicated as the Mary Lily Flagler Manse. It currently serves as offices and classroom space for the church.

Rubye Lee Beydler Moeller commented on the close friendships between Brubaker and her own husband Billie as well as Billy McGuire. She noted they all had good clean fun. They, with other notables to include Arthur Lee Campbell, John Spengler, Pete and Polly Pierce and Putnam Calhoun, found their way through hard times by keeping active and enjoying each other's company. Mrs. Moeller also commented that she and Brubaker used to entertain together, he on his beloved violin and she on piano.

November 14, 1991

The Mary Lily Flagler Manse remains intact as Edward Brubaker remembered, and still serves as church offices and meeting rooms.

MOCCASIN BRANCH
Ambrose Masters

Every year the annual Moccasin Branch Fair is organized by the parishioners of St. Ambrose Catholic Church, seen above. I spoke with Ambrose Masters, who has lived in or near Moccasin Branch since his birth in 1900. He remembers helping build the present parish church in 1907. Although only seven years of age, he hitched the horse for his father and helped him deliver materials to the church. The information supplied by the storyteller, who preferred to remain anonymous when this tale was originally told, is rich with history about this section of the county.

The first thing we had to do in preparation for the fair was to catch the gophers. I'll bet you don't even know what a gopher is. Well, it's a great big land tortoise that we catch and cook up into gopher stew. We always had that and maybe some chicken perlieu for dinner at the fair. Of course, we can't do that anymore because it's against the law to kill the gophers now. It's an endangered species, don't you see.

Anyway, we would hunt the gophers up on Circle Square Ranch on Route 200 out of Ocala. We had permission to go. They liked to get them out of there because of the horses. When they were moving the cattle they might step in a hole and might hurt somebody or hurt the horses. We used to get a hundred or so for the fair. We would have to feed about a thousand people or maybe more.

I remember one time when we were getting ready to go on a hunt someone played a prank. I don't remember exactly who went that time except I know L.O. Davis and Sub Rogero were there. This man (I don't remember his name) ran a hardware store on the corner of Hypolita and Cordova Streets and we were all going to Ocala in his truck. Well, this boy Duley Lopez was going with us. His mother made him a chocolate cake to take on the gopher hunt and she put it in a cheese box—you know, the wooden cheese boxes. We always took our lunch with us and Duley was particularly anxious to cut into that cake. Well, we don't know how that old gopher lifted the lid to that box and got in, but he did. When Duley lifted the lid to the box he was a very disappointed person, you know. He wanted to beat L.O. up about that because he thought L.O. was the one that did it. I don't know who did it—never did find out for sure. L.O. swore he didn't. Anyway we all got back to fishing for gophers after lunch, but I don't think Duley ever got over the gopher in his cake.

You fish for gophers with a pole, you know. You get a long pole, something about twenty feet or more that's flexible—something you can handle. Most times the hole isn't straight, probably for protection. Also if they hit a root they are going to go around it, don't you see. You don't use any bait or anything like that. You hook the shell in the back. When you feel the gopher, you turn your hook up. Sometimes the gopher will be facing you and you'll catch them in the front. When the side is to you it's difficult to catch them because there isn't anything to hook on to. They have a mound around the hole they dug and sometimes the hole is so deep you can't reach the gopher with an ordinary pole. But you feel that gopher. You know what it is. It's not like a root. It's like something solid—there is a different sound to it. Sometimes you can catch them easy, but sometimes they are hard to pull out.

This time at Circle Square Range I had hooked a gopher but I couldn't pull it. I kept pulling and pulling, but that ol' gopher had eased himself off and I had hooked a rock. That might have been the time Father O'Donavan went. He would often go with us. We had the priest, we had the sheriff, we had the undertaker. I don't know if we had a doctor or not, but we had everybody else. We went on for many years, but we can't do it anymore. It was a good outing. We'd always get a hundred or more. It was a big job cleaning them. The fair was generally held within a few days.

I guess we would clean them right away. You have to scald them first to get the skin off. Then they have toenails on their feet—you cut that off. The front paws have a hard crust you have to cut off, too. They would be washed two or three times and sometimes they'd be kept in the freezer two or three days. When I cooked them here, or my wife cooked, we would cook them plain. We didn't like the thyme and bay leaves and all that junk. I didn't like the taste of all that. The main thing you put in would be salt and black pepper and datil peppers or course. Datil peppers are local grown peppers. They must have been brought here by the Spaniards or somebody many years

Ambrose Masters (front row, fourth from left), stands with classmates. *Courtesy St. Ambrose Parish*

ago. It's a very hot thing. It has a flavor all its own. We never used green peppers. We just used datil peppers. Then you add potatoes or carrots like beef stew. You had to cook the gophers a long time to tender it. The potatoes don't take as long to cook so you add them later. Sometimes the stew was very good and sometimes it wasn't all that good. Some people would come just for the stew.

I suppose the fairs started before I was born. I can remember back to 1907—that was when they were building the church. Now there was another church here before St. Ambrose. This was the second church. The original masses were said in the first church. Some of the lumber from the original church was used in the present church and in the schoolhouse, too. The bell was in the original church, too. It was baptized like a person. Originally they had a handmade wheel with a rope fastened to it. Occasionally someone would pull it too hard and turn it over and someone would have to right it so you could ring it again. Sometime after I moved into this house—in 1934—that wheel just disintegrated and we had to do something to ring the bell. Father Langlade used to ring the angelus three times a day, morning, noon and night. A friend of mine and I made a piece of metal and put it up there with bolts so the bell would ring again. We fixed it so it would go from side to side and not turn. It had a nice tone to it.

You have to understand that all the families here knew each other and raised their families together. I was born and raised right across the roadway from Dave Simms and his wife. His sister married Bartolo Solona, who lived right over here. These people were all very close together. Across Moccasin Branch over there was the Weedman family and Joe Solana. Uncle Bartolo and Uncle Philip lived down where Spuds is now. The Weedmans lived out by Molasses Junction and the Rogeros lived out across the branch. Uncle Philip and Uncle Bartolo married Lopezes. They were all farmers and had to live off the land. They raised hogs and cattle and farmed too. So you can see how the fair was always a big family event. It has been a tradition since before I can remember. For some of us I guess fishing for gophers was as much fun as eating the stew.

Ambrose Masters was born December 7, 1900, and died October 12, 1996. According to *The Branches: Springs of Living Water*, a publication of the St. Ambrose Parish, the annual fair started well before 1888. A newspaper article of that year reports that visitors came in carts, buggies and on horseback, with two "carloads" arriving by rail.

Gopher fishing was obviously important to many members of the community, as illustrated by a 1954 review. Listed as tackling the important job were A.J. Hartley, Quentin Brubaker, Francis Brubaker, Hugh Rogero, Carmen Brubaker, Gus Craig Jr. and L.O. Davis. No priest is mentioned for this outing, but the sheriff (Davis) and undertaker (Craig Jr.) are there.

March 17, 1988

The St. Ambrose Fair remains a strong tradition with or without gopher stew.